WESTMONT HIGH SCHOOL LIBRARY

W9-CSZ-888

WESTMONT HIGH SCHOOL

T 20978

DATE DUE

OCL 27 05			
SEP 22 '70			

796.357   29731
Kee

Keene, Kerry

1960: the last pure
season

GAYLORD M2

796.357
kee

962

@ 0.02

1960: The Last Pure Season

by
Kerry Keene

Sports Publishing Inc.
www.SportsPublishingInc.com

WESTMONT HIGH SCHOOL LIBRARY
CAMPBELL UNION HIGH SCHOOL DISTRICT
IBRARY BOOK No. 29731

© 2000 Kerry Keene

Director of production: Susan M. McKinney
Cover design: Julie L. Denzer
Production assistant: Crystal Gummere
Proofreader: Jennifer R. Gill-Green

ISBN: 1-58261-280-3
Library of Congress Catalog Card Number: 00-100039

SPORTS PUBLISHING INC.
804 N. Neil
Champaign, IL 61820
www.sportspublishinginc.com

Printed in the United States.

To Pam, who is my greatest ally in the completion of such endeavors.

*And to all those guys across America, now in their early fifties,
for whom baseball was a truly magical place back in 1960.*

Contents

Acknowledgments

My most valuable player in this project is esteemed member of the Society for American Baseball Research Richard Thompson. His gracious, unlimited access to his extremely noteworthy collection of research materials was an absolutely invaluable resource.

Other SABR members who lent a hand include Dick Clark, head of the Negro League's Committee; Bill Ryzcek, David Gough, Steve Gietschier of *The Sporting News*; and Dick Johnson of the Sports Museum of New England.

Thanks go to several members of the staff at the National Baseball Hall of Fame and Museum, including Eric Enders, William Francis, Bill Burdick, and Frank Simio; to the staff at the Boston Public Library's Microtext Department; to Brian Parkinson of Topps Inc. for allowing photos of Topps baseball cards to be published; and to Dick Sarkisian of The Sports Tradition collectibles and memorabilia shop in West Bridgewater, Massachusetts for graciously allowing cards from his personal collection to be photographed.

It is difficult to imagine undertaking a project of this type without having access to microfilm of all 52 issues of *The Sporting News* from 1960. The single richest resource for information of this kind, it allowed me to relive the year at my own slow pace.

Thanks to my previous partners Ray Sinibaldi and David Hickey for being sounding boards and for helping to lead me down the path in the first place on which I now find myself. Here's hoping we will work together again.

And my appreciation to 1960 National League Most Valuable Player Dick Groat, for sharing his personal memories of that spectacular and most unusual year.

Foreword

Reflecting back to that special moment, I can picture it as if it were yesterday. It was the seventh game of the 1960 World Series, the start of the bottom of the ninth inning with the score tied at nine. I was scheduled to bat fourth in the inning, and had just grabbed my bat out of the bat rack and put on my batting helmet.

Suddenly, lead off hitter Bill Mazeroski launched the second pitch from Yankee Ralph Terry high toward the left field wall as we stood stunned, not believing what we were seeing. As the ball cleared the ivy-covered wall, it was the most special moment I had been part of on a baseball field. As a Pittsburgh-area native who had attended countless games at Forbes Field as a youngster, I was privileged to be part of the Pirates' first world championship in 35 years. It was the greatest thrill I've ever had.

I was blessed to be associated with such an extraordinary group of individuals both on and off the field. Roberto Clemente possessed the greatest God-given talent I ever saw on a baseball field. As a shortstop, I had the tremedous fortune to play beside Mazeroski, the greatest defensive second baseman I've ever seen. Elroy Face was one of the very best relief pitchers, and if he and Maz had played for New York or Los Angeles, they both would have been elected to the Hall of Fame long ago. I would be remiss if I did not acknowledge the 1960 Cy Young Award winner and consummate gentleman, Vern Law, left fielder Bob Skinner, and Bill Virdon, my roommate on the road for seven seasons.

The camaraderie I shared with these men still exists to this day. As members of the Pittsburgh Pirates Alumni Association, one of the strongest of its kind, we are able to remain close, as well as engage in many charitable endeavors.

When baseball's All-Century team was introduced during the 1999 World Series, it was a source of pride to know that I had competed with or against several of the honorees. To have played on the same field as Stan Musial, Willie Mays, Hank Aaron, Mickey Mantle, Sandy Koufax, and especially Ted Williams, was a privilege.

Also, I was fortunate to have George Sisler as our batting instructor back around the time of our championship. As one of the truly great hitters of the 1920s and an esteemed member of the Hall of Fame, I give him all the credit in the world for any success I had as a hitter.

I am very proud to have played back in that era—one that I truly consider a "Golden Age of Baseball." It was so much more of a team game, as opposed to playing for individual glory. On that '60 Pirates team, we almost felt as though we'd die and go to hell if we left a runner stranded on third. We also had a very nice relationship with the fans, with virtually none of the hostilities that seem to exist today. We actually knew a lot of the steady fans who sat in the box-seats on a first-name basis. As for my salary back then, I made $18,000 in 1960, and I never had the vaguest idea how much any of my teammates were making, nor was I concerned. There also appears to be a noticeable dilution of talent in the majors today, with players spread throughout 30 teams. If there were 16, or even 20 teams as there was back in my era, no doubt the quality of play would be far better.

Here in the Pittsburgh area, it seems that anyone over 45 years old still raves about the 1960 season. In my 14-year baseball career, it remains my most special. From a baseball standpoint, it was certainly a year well worth documenting.

Dick Groat
1960 National League MVP

Introduction

Surveying the landscape of major league baseball on the threshold of the 21st Century is sure to create feelings of ambivalence to longtime followers of the game. It continues to be an eminently enjoyable game, with an abundance of exciting and talented performers. There is, as is true of almost any time in the game's history, no shortage of figures currently active who will one day end up with their likeness cast in bronze and displayed in Cooperstown.

Yet, examining the makeup of today's game, the veteran fan is struck by many differences from that which he grew to love decades ago. So many teams, so many players, so much freedom of movement, and of course, so much money.

In 1961, the American League began the era of expansion by adding the Los Angeles Angels and the new edition of Washington Senators, increasing the season schedule to 162 games in the process. The following season, the National League followed suit by welcoming aboard the New York Mets and Houston Colt .45's. Gone forever were the old eight-team leagues that both the American and National Leagues had maintained continuously for 60 years.

That, of course was just the beginning. Nineteen sixty-nine saw four more new teams added to the fold—the San Diego Padres and Montreal Expos joining the NL, with the Kansas City Royals and ill-fated Seattle Pilots added to the AL. The two leagues had now swelled to 12 teams apiece, prompting them to abandon the traditional one-division format in favor of two six-team divisions in each circuit. This also created the extra round of play-offs to determine the league champion.

Simply finishing in first place and going directly to the World Series was never again to be the way.

In 1977, the AL acted alone, giving Seattle another try with the Mariners, and Canada's second team, the Toronto Blue Jays. The NL took its turn in 1993, welcoming the Colorado Rockies and the Florida Marlins into the fold. And lastly, two more teams were declared "major league" in 1998—the Arizona Diamondbacks in the NL and Tampa Bay Devil

Rays in the AL to bring the total to a whopping 30 teams. One can only speculate when and where the inevitable next round of expansion will occur.

The increase in the past 40 years from 16 to 30 teams has created an additional 350 roster spots. While the talent pool has also grown larger, most would argue that it has not grown large enough to stock all teams with top quality, major league talent. The state of pitching in the late 1990s, exacerbated by the use of five-man rotations would seem to support this belief of a "watered-down product".

So many teams, so many players.

How easy it was to follow the game, and to know the teams and their players back in the pre-expansion era. Eight teams in the American, eight in the National. A full schedule of action in the major leagues would yield only eight box scores to examine in the newspaper the following morning! Committing to memory the starting line-ups in the league of one's hometown team was not a particularly daunting task. To attempt the equivalent today would seem to require nearly full-time study.

So much freedom, so much money.

When the federal courts granted baseball players free agency in 1975, it made possible the nomadic, mercenary performer we see much of today. One result of this was that the nucleus of a given team would not stay intact nearly as long as it once might. It seems now to take well into the season to become fully adjusted to roster changes and where all of the most recent crop of free agents have landed.

Whereas in 1960 it was virtually unheard of for a player to have an agent representing him in contract negotiations, it is nearly unheard of for a player not to be represented in today's free agent market. There are many factors that have led to the immense escalation in player salaries over the past few decades, and the presence of agents would certainly be among them.

Disproportionately, escalating salaries have created increasing disillusionment for the old-time patrons of the game. In 1960, the highest-paid ballplayers earned roughly 25 times that of the average adult American male. Today, that figure exceeds 400 times!

Granted, revenues generated have increased dramatically as well, but a single baseball player being compensated with $15 million per year does not tend to sit well with the essential but unsung professionals such as the police officers, firefighters, nurses, and schoolteachers of today. Two of the game's brightest stars, Ted Williams and Stan Musial—legends in their own time, requested, and received pay cuts going into the '60 season due to sub-par seasons in '59.

Said Musial at the time: "The Cardinals have been generous to me in the past few years, so I thought I'd be kind to them." Willie Mays, discussing his contract in February of 1960 stated: "I never worry about those things. I leave it up to (Giants owner) Horace Stoneham. He calls me, tells me what I'm getting, and I sign. It's been that way ever since I joined the club." Hank Aaron has gone on record as saying he wouldn't trade the earlier days of his career for the millions players now make, and also added that the competition was much greater then than it is now.

These are not approaches that are seen or expected from today's breed of ballplayer. Needless to say, the agents or Player's Union would simply not allow it. It is also worth recalling that the vast majority of big league ballplayers actually worked "regular jobs" in the off-season back in 1960!

Any given season will feature players who will eventually rise to legendary status, and 1960 could very likely hold its own with any other in this regard. Scanning the major league rosters of that storied campaign reveals household names such as Ted Williams, Mickey Mantle, Mays, Aaron, Musial, and Roberto Clemente, just to name a few. Active at that time were nine of 16 members of the 500 home run club. The outfield was a particularly rich area. When *The Sporting News* released its list of the top 100 players of the 20th Century in late 1998, seven of the top ten outfielders selected were competing in the majors at the dawn of the 1960s.

It seems that a very good case could be made that the quality of play and overall level of talent in the major leagues in 1960 was at its highest than any time before or since. For with Jackie Robinson having opened the door for black players 13 years prior, the big leagues were now, for all practical purposes, fully integrated. The Boston Red Sox were the final team to add a black player, doing so in 1959, and by '60 the Red Sox roster included three. It is undeniable that Organized Baseball did itself a great disservice by not allowing the Willie Mayses and Hank Aarons of an earlier time to participate before the late 1940s. Ty Cobb, Walter Johnson, Babe Ruth et al simply were not competing against the absolute best available talent. That could not be said of Mantle, Warren Spahn, or Brooks Robinson in 1960. Nearly ninety black players appeared in the majors in 1960. For the first time in history, no player was being denied the opportunity based on the color of his skin.

This high-point in quality of play the game had achieved by 1960 slipped back the next season with the addition of two new teams—50 new big-league roster spots, and the watering-down process was underway. Fifty more the next year, 100 more seven years later, and so on, and the game has maybe never really fully recovered.

So, as a cartoon character of many years back might have said " . . . turn the Way-Back machine to 1960", where the terms designated hitter, domed stadium, artificial turf, free agency, and wild-card were not a part of the lexicon; where baseball, experiencing a truly "Golden Age", was undoubtedly the "National Pastime", surpassing in popularity the NFL, NBA, and NHL combined; where the highest-priced ticket in the entire sport were the $3.50 box seats in Yankee Stadium and Dodger Stadium.

Take the car keys, go out into the driveway, and jump into the spanking new 1960 Chevy Impala on a sunny Sunday afternoon. Turn on the radio and tune in the ballgame. Take a trip back to one of Baseball's most historic and pivotal years—a year when the near formation of a new third major league that would have been treated as an equal of the existing American and National Leagues very likely would have sent the game off in quite a different direction. Arguably, there had never before been a year that had witnessed so many significant events and monumental decisions that would impact the game so profoundly.

Entering the new century seems a fitting time to go back 40 years and take such a nostalgic journey.

Chapter One

Setting the Stage

The upcoming season of 1960 would be one of milestones of the two major league circuits, with the American League celebrating its 60th campaign, the National its 85th. The Baseball Writers Association of America (BBWAA) took this fitting time to look back deep into the past to bestow a long overdue, richly deserved honor.

Once the most fiercely determined, dominating player to ever grace a ball field, a 73-year-old Ty Cobb, was now bent, frail, and slowly dying. On January 31 at the annual New York Baseball Writers Dinner held at the Astor Hotel, the BBWAA presented Cobb with the Player of the Year award for 1911. Longtime New York baseball writer Dan Daniel also presented him with the Louisville Slugger Silver Bat award for having captured that season's title with a lofty .420 average. Neither of these awards had existed 49 years prior.

The popular notion, exacerbated by the 1995 film "Cobb", depicts him as a completely out-of-control lunatic in the last years of his life. Yet his demeanor upon accepting these awards in January of 1960 was decidedly different. In obvious pain but good spirits, Cobb graciously told the crowd, "I'm proud to have been a ballplayer."

He stated that one of his greatest thrills in life was to be able to build a hospital in his hometown of Royston, Georgia, along with establishing an educational foundation. The 1,500 in attendance roared in approval. After the dinner, Cobb told a reporter, "I should get down on my hands and knees and thank the game for what it has done for me."

A few weeks later, one of baseball's holy shrines experienced a very poignant final chapter. On February 23, the demolition of Brooklyn's Ebbetts Field began, with 200 faithful "mourners" gathered for the somber occasion. Before the actual dismantling began, a brief ceremony was held, emceed by Red Barber's former broadcast partner Art Helfer. Former Dodger P.A. announcer Tex Rickard also spoke, and wheelchair-bound Roy Campanella accepted an urn of dirt from the homeplate area. He recalled for those in attendance that the last game Brooklyn ever played there was also the last game he appeared in before his tragic auto accident which followed a little over three months later.

As the ceremony came to a close, demolition officially began when a two-ton iron ball painted to look like a baseball crashed down on the visitors dugout. The six-acre site would soon be the new home of a middle-income housing project. One observer on this day sadly stated, "That's progress." Another replied, "If that's progress, they can have it."

In a further note on progress, less than two months later on April 13 on the other side of the country, the contract to build Dodger Stadium was awarded to Vinelli Constructors.

As for a small part of Ebbetts Field living on, 1,500 of its seats were shipped down to the Dodger Spring Training complex in Vero Beach, Florida and installed in Holman Stadium.

Another sad event occurred several weeks later, when Kansas City Athletics owner Arnold M. Johnson died suddenly on March 10, shortly after watching his team play an intra-squad game. Johnson, who had owned Yankee Stadium prior to purchasing the Athletics in 1954, had just observed that for the first time since buying the team, there might be cause for optimism on the field in 1960. He left to drive to his winter home in Palm Beach, and suffered a massive cerebral hemorrhage on the way. His death would put the Athletics ownership situation in doubt, and ultimately pave the way for Charles O. Finley to purchase the team later in the year. Just two weeks after Johnson's death, a group of New Jersey businessmen made an unsuccessful attempt to buy the team and move them to that state.

There were several off-season transactions that placed many noteworthy players in new uniforms for the upcoming season. In December of 1959, the Yankees sent popular veteran Hank Bauer, along with Don Larsen, Norm Seibern, and "Marvelous" Marv Throneberry to Kansas City for 25-year-old Roger Maris and two others. The Yankees felt that Maris's ability to pull the ball might be utilized best with their short right field. It is unlikely that even they would imagine just how much he would help them in the next three seasons. White Sox manager Al Lopez commented that he was not quite convinced of Maris's potential, and at the beginning of Spring Training stated that Norm Seibern would hit more home runs for the A's than Maris would for New York. Lopez missed badly on his prediction. In a similar amount of at-bats that season, Seibern had less than half of Maris's total of 39.

One of the true blockbuster trades of the era occurred on April 17, just two days before the curtain rose on the American League's regular season. Young Indians right fielder Rocky Colavito, the AL co-leader in home runs the season before and a truly beloved figure in Cleveland, was swapped for '59 batting champion Harvey Kuenn of Detroit. Rocking the baseball world, it marked the first time in history that a league's home run champ was exchanged for its batting champ.

Colavito had been holding out, refusing to sign the contract the Indians had offered him, and general manager Frank Lane said in early February that he would consider trading him for Kuenn. Finally, as Spring Training was set to begin, Colavito settled with

Roger Maris of the Yankees and Hank Bauer of Kansas City. The two players had been traded for each other in the off-season, and inspect their new uniforms upon meeting in Spring Training for the first time in 1960. (National Baseball Library)

Cleveland, signing a $35,000 contract for 1960. At that time, Lane boldly predicted, "Rocky is going to beat Ruth's 60!" But as the Spring wore on, a 22-year-old, 6'7", 225 lb. slugging outfielder named Walt Bond began to emerge in the Indians' camp. In the end, Lane and manager Joe Gordon felt Colavito became expendable due to the power potential of the rookie Bond. In Kuenn, they were acquiring a hitter who was considerably more adept at getting on base, and also regarded as a slightly better outfielder. His .314 lifetime batting average was second among active players to Ted Williams' .346., yet it took a while for the furor to die down in Cleveland. In early May, with Colavito now a member of the Tigers, Lane had amended his opinion on Rocky's power potential to break Ruth's record, now saying he could do it only, "if he didn't try to hit one over the fence every time he came to bat."

One interesting aspect of the contract Colavito had signed with the Indians came to light shortly after the trade. Lane had included a bonus of $1,000 if Rocky did NOT hit 40 home runs, reasoning that he would be more valuable if he wasn't always swinging for the fences. After the trade, Colavito asked the Tigers' DeWitt if the bonus was still in effect. DeWitt paid him the $1,000 and told him to keep swinging for the fences.

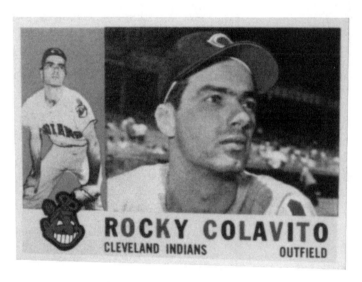

Rocky Colavito—1960 Topps card # 400. The immensely popular right fielder's trade to Detroit just before Opening Day sent shockwaves throughout Cleveland. Many loyal Indians fans threatened to stay away from the ballpark in protest. Subsequent editorials referred to him as "an institution in the wigwam," and "the type of fellow any older fan would love to have as a son." (Courtesy, Topps Inc.)

The Indians had also been involved in a seemingly minor deal five days before the Colavito trade, but which turned out to be one of the more lopsided ever made. They sent first baseman Norm Cash, whom they'd just received from Chicago in December of '59 to Detroit in exchange for minor league third baseman Steve Demeter. Cash went on to hit a total of 373 home runs for the Tigers over the next 15 seasons, while Demeter appeared in four games for Cleveland in '60, then completely fell off the major league map. General manager Lane likely came to regret his quote from just before Spring Training when he said, "I'd like to steal Steve Demeter from the Tigers. He's as good looking a right handed hitter as you ever want to see."

Minnie Minoso, probably the finest all-around left fielder in the AL in the decade of the '50s was reacquired by the White Sox from the Indians. The Cuban star had spent from 1951 through '57 with Chicago before going to Cleveland for two seasons, and would now be manning his old post for the AL champ White Sox. Manager Lopez stated that he hoped Minoso would provide 20-25 homers and 90-100 RBI, and Minnie did not disappoint.

Longtime Phillies lead off hitter Richie Ashburn was sent to the Cubs in January. The Philly fan favorite had dropped off significantly in '59, and Chicago hoped he could regain his batting form.

There were serious questions regarding the game's two most revered stars as training camps opened in 1960. Ted Williams and Stan Musial were clearly in the very twilight of their storied careers, which was cause for considerable speculation on the part of sportswriters. Ted was plagued by a variety of ailments, including a bad leg, shoulder soreness, and a nagging neck injury. Retirement before Opening Day was a very real possibility.

As for Musial, he was coming off his worst season yet in his 18-year career. In '59 he had uncharacteristically posted just 14 homers, 44 RBI, and a .255 batting average—55 points lower than his previous low. Musial himself admitted that he had taken it far

Ted Williams—Whom The Sporting News *would hail in the Summer of 1960 as the Player of the Decade for the 1950s. Nineteen sixty was rife with speculation regarding his baseball future. (Courtesy, The Sports Museum of New England)*

too easy in Spring Training of '59, and when the regular season began, he just never got going. During the winter of '59-'60, he had dedicated himself to a rigorous workout routine and was pushing himself hard in Spring Training. He made a good showing in the practice games and was determined to come back strong.

With Williams' and Musial's days of batting domination behind them, baseball was seeing the emergence of several young hitters seemingly on the verge of taking their places. Mays and Mantle, both 28-year-olds at the start of the '60 season headed a stellar group that also included Hank Aaron, Roberto Clemente, Al Kaline, Frank Robinson, Ernie Banks, and Vada Pinson, to name a few. Charlie Dressen, new manager of the Milwaukee Braves said of Aaron just before Spring Training began, "He should be the next .400 hitter. He's as good as any I've seen in my 41 years in baseball."

Cincinnati outfielder Pinson, just 21 years old but entering his third season, was thought by some to be the "next Willie Mays". Like Mays, he was skilled in all phases of the game, but it was his speed that particularly impressed observers. Pinson was considered the fastest in the NL at going from first to third on a single, and after an exhibition game between the Reds and Tigers on March 26, 1960, Detroit players voted he was, "faster than Mantle" based on his performance that day.

Perhaps the young slugger garnering the most publicity that Spring was Dodger rookie Frank Howard. Chief Dodger scout Al Campanis said in January that the 6'7", 255 lb. Howard was "the man who will break Babe Ruth's home run mark," and added, "He can hit the ball farther than any man in the game." Early in training camp, Duke Snider cautioned that it was unfair to make big predictions on Howard's home run potential, and said, "He thinks he has to hit a 600-foot homer every time up." The Dodgers were actually considering the possibility in the Spring of switching long-time first baseman Gil Hodges to third base to make room for Howard, who normally played the outfield. It all became academic when Howard was demoted to Spokane just before Opening Day, partly to learn the strike zone, partly to learn a little humility. In a short time he would learn both and come back to the Dodgers to make quite a splash.

As Opening Day of '60 was fast approaching, baseball writers across the country were engaging in the time-honored tradition of predicting the outcome of the league standings. A poll was taken amongst BBWAA members, with 266 writers participating in forecasting the eventual World Series opponents. San Francisco was the popular choice to capture the NL flag, with the White Sox picked to repeat in the AL. Braves manager Dressen tried his hand at predicting the outcome in his typically agitating manner, and started a feud with the World Champion Dodgers in the process. Dressen, who served as a coach for the Dodgers the year before, said tauntingly, "If Los Angeles is the only club we have to worry about, then we've got no worries." This drew the ire of several Dodgers, including Carl Furillo, Sandy Koufax, and '59 Series MVP Larry Sherry.

As for the Pittsburgh Pirates, not many were taking their pennant chances too seriously. The general feeling was that a shortage of top pitching and a lack of power would keep them out of the race. One notable exception was highly controversial New York writer Dick Young, who picked them to top the senior circuit.

Over in the American League, the Yankee dynasty of the 1950s was seemingly losing some of its luster. The comment heard most often throughout training camps in the Spring of 1960 was, "We're no longer afraid of the Yankees." Many of the top executives in the AL, including president Joe Cronin, Bill Veeck, Tom Yawkey, Lee MacPhail, and others, believed that the era of Yankees invincibility was over, and the race was wide open. Manager Casey Stengel knew the pressure was on and went on record as saying he would resign if his team didn't get to the World Series. The team's 11-21 record in Spring Training cast a further shadow of doubt over their chances.

One long-anticipated event that was to occur on Opening Day was the debut of the Giants' new state-of-the-art facility; Candlestick Park. The team was leaving behind old Seals Stadium, their home since migrating from New York's Polo Grounds after the 1957 season. Built in the shadows of Bay View Hill, Candlestick was the most carefully planned, modern ballpark in existence. The first major league park to be built entirely of reinforced concrete, it featured the country's largest electronic scoreboard.

Nineteen sixty was a year of beginnings and of endings. For the franchise located in the nation's capital, it was the beginning of the end.

Chapter Two

An Abundance of Fame in the Game

There are many who are of the opinion that Willie Howard Mays was the most skilled all-around player to have ever played the game. When *The Sporting News* published its list of the top 100 players of the 20th Century in late 1998, only "the Babe" himself was ranked higher. The Associated Press conducted a similar poll with the same results. Going into the 1960 season, the 28-year-old center fielder had eight major league seasons under his belt, in which time he had won the Rookie of the Year award (1951); Most Valuable Player award (1954); was named to six All-Star teams; helped the Giants win two NL championships and one World Championship; won the Rawlings Gold Glove award in its first three years of existence ('57, '58 and '59); and led the NL in stolen bases each of the previous four seasons ('56 through '59). In short, Mays was smack dab in the middle of a career that would later prompt the century-plus old publication to regard him as just one home run slugging freak of nature away from being the greatest ballplayer who ever lived. From his trademark basket catches to his distinct bow-legged running style to his joyous enthusiasm for the game, the young Mays was the very embodiment of the game as it was in 1960.

Giants superstar Willie Mays. Dodgers coach Bobby Bragan said of Mays in September of 1960, "Mays is the greatest player I've ever seen. He could make the All-Star team at every position except pitcher and catcher, and I'm not too certain he couldn't do it there either." Bragan was quoted several months later as saying that he had the same quality as Jackie Robinson "...when he gets on base, opposing players don't think about the next hitter, but worry about him." Alvin Dark said in early November, "I've been in the National League since 1946. There's no one I've seen in baseball who can do the things he can."

True aficionados of the game and its near 130-year major league history have a deep appreciation for observing the highest caliber of play. When a given player is able to maintain such a level for a large portion of a long career, his image on the field becomes etched in the minds of those who repeatedly witnessed his talents. Some such players will attain a legendary status in the annals of this so-called "National Pastime" that is cemented when their likeness is cast in bronze, forever to be displayed in the National Baseball Hall of Fame.

No less than 51 individuals who were directly involved in some capacity within Major League Baseball during the 1960 season have been so inducted into the Cooperstown, New York shrine. From active players, to managers, to coaches, executives, and umpires, the game was positively flooded with figures who would go on to achieve that special status. The roll call shows a veritable Who's Who of baseball of the mid-20th Century.

Joining Mays in this group of active baseball immortals are the following:

Ted Williams—Left field, Boston Red Sox. It had been 21 years since this brash, skinny, 20-year-old arrived on the scene. By this, his final season, he had, in the opinion of many, fulfilled his dream of being regarded as the greatest hitter who ever lived.

Stan Musial—Outfield/First Base, St. Louis Cardinals. Entering the new decade, the 38-year-old Cardinal's career was winding down, but he stood as the only active member of the 3,000 hit club. "The Man" was also the active leader in games, at-bats, total bases, extra base hits, runs, doubles, and triples, as well as being the NL leader in homers among his contemporaries.

Hank Aaron—Right field, Milwaukee Braves. Was well on his way to displaying the remarkable consistency and durability that would be his trademark. The "Hammer" had missed a total of

Stan Musial, longtime St. Louis Cardinals superstar. On April 29 of '60 he became the first player in history to play 1,000 games at two different positions, first base and outfield. On July 17, he reached an offensive milestone by surpassing Nap Lajoie to move into fifth on the all-time hit list with 3,252 hits.

only six games the previous five seasons, and reached the 40-home run plateau in '60—a figure he would reach eight times.

Mickey Mantle—Center field, New York Yankees. With his 1960 World Series appearance against the Pirates, The Mick had now played in eight Fall Classics in his ten seasons in the majors. Led the AL in homers in '60, edging his new teammate, Roger Maris, by one.

Warren Spahn—Pitcher, Milwaukee Braves. Longtime Braves left-hander was in the process of becoming baseball's winningest lefty in history after not winning his first game until the age of 25. Led NL in wins in '60 with 21, including his first no-hitter.

Ernie Banks—Shortstop, Chicago Cubs. 1960 saw Banks, for the fifth time in six seasons have both over 40 homers and over 100 RBI. This was the last season that Banks was exclusively a shortstop, as he would begin the transition to first base the following year.

Ernie Banks and Mickey Mantle. The home run champions of 1960 in each league, Banks totaled 41, Mantle 40. The two sluggers posed here at the All-Star game.

Yogi Berra—Catcher, New York Yankees. Had begun to spend more time in left field and less time behind the plate, giving way to Elston Howard. Appearing in the '60 Series, he had now seen action in 11 Fall Classics, more than any other player to that point. Yogi had appeared in 68 of the 86 world series games played from 1947 through 1960.

Eddie Mathews—Third Base, Milwaukee Braves. Practically redefined third base as a power position, slugging 40 or more home runs four times in the 1950s. The NL home run champ of '59 came back in '60 with 39 round-trippers and 124 RBI.

Whitey Ford—Pitcher, New York Yankees. The AL's premier left-hander entered the season with a 121-50 lifetime record and concluded it with two complete-game shutouts in the World Series against Pittsburgh.

Frank Robinson—First Base/Left field, Cincinnati Reds. The NL's '56 Rookie of the Year was just entering his prime as one of the game's bright young superstars. Pounded 31 homers and led the NL in slugging percentage at .595.

Duke Snider—Center field, Los Angeles Dodgers. Led the majors in home runs in the 1950s with 326. Had hit the last of his 11 world series homers in the sixth and final game of the 1959 Series to help L.A. clinch.

Early Wynn—Pitcher, Chicago White Sox. Had earned the Cy Young award in 1959 at the age of 39. Compiled a record of only 13-12 in '60, but tied for the AL lead in shutouts with four.

Robin Roberts—Pitcher, Philadelphia Phillies. One of the truly dominant pitchers of the '50s with six straight 20-win seasons ('50 through '55), followed by a 19-win season. At 34 years old in

The 1956 National League Rookie of the Year would add many more honors and distinctions to his resume, including two MVP awards, a triple crown award, two world championships, and becoming the first black manager in the majors.

'60, he was beginning to taper off (12-16, 4.02 ERA), but was effective enough to maintain a 3 1/2-to-1 strikeout-to-walk-ratio.

Nellie Fox—Second Base, Chicago White Sox. Without a doubt the AL's top second baseman of the 1950s. Had a consecutive-game streak of 798 that was stopped on September 4, 1960, due to a virus. Was the league's reigning MVP going into '60.

Al Kaline—Right field, Detroit Tigers. Coming off a '59 season that saw him lead the AL in slugging percentage, and become one of the youngest players in history to reach his 1,000th hit. Recorded his career high in stolen bases in '60 with 19.

Nellie Fox—Manager Al Lopez described him as the ideal type of player. "A hustler who plays for the club and not himself. A fellow who moves the baserunners around and doesn't strike out very often." Fox achieved his 2,000th hit on July 24 and saw his 798 consecutive game streak end on September 4 of '60. (National Baseball Library)

Don Drysdale—Pitcher, Los Angeles Dodgers. Had been regarded as the Dodgers ace since 1957—their last year in Brooklyn. Led NL in strikeouts in '60 for second straight year.

Don Drysdale's 246 strikeouts in 1960 were the highest total in the NL since Dazzy Vance's 262 in 1924. One NL writer took a poll of hitters in the summer of '60 to determine which pitchers in the league threw the fastest. Drysdale won the poll, while Koufax and Dick Farrell of the Phillies tied for second. (National Baseball Library)

Roberto Clemente—Right field, Pittsburgh Pirates. Helped Pittsburgh win its first NL pennant in 33 years in '60. This was his breakthrough season, his sixth in the majors, reaching career highs to that point in batting, home runs, and RBI.

Richie Ashburn—Center field, Chicago Cubs. One of the most outstanding center fielders of his time, with over 500 putouts on four occasions. After 12 seasons with the Phillies, winning batting titles in '55 and '58, he was traded to the Cubs in January of '60.

Jim Bunning—Pitcher, Detroit Tigers. Tough competitor with a sidearm delivery. Had tough luck in '60 with an 11-14 record, experiencing very poor run support, but the AL's second-best ERA at 2.79. Led the league in strikeouts for the second year in a row.

Harmon Killebrew—First Base/Third Base, Washington Senators. Coming off his breakout season of '59 in which he slugged 42 homers. Made his first appearance at first base after primarily playing third. Embarked on a decade ('60-'69) in which he totaled 393 home runs.

Red Schoendienst—Second Base, Milwaukee Braves. Had been named to ten All-Star teams. Was in the midst of a 45-consecutive season span of wearing a major league uniform as either player, manager, or coach. Was making a comeback this season from a bout with tuberculosis.

Hoyt Wilhelm—Pitcher, Baltimore Orioles. Primarily a relief specialist, the knuckleballer was coming off a '59 season that saw him utilized almost exclusively as a starter for the only time in his 21-year career. In the Spring of '60, Orioles manager Paul Richards said of Wilhelm, "It's conceivable he can pitch till he's 45 because of his easy motion."

Luis Aparicio—Shortstop, Chicago White Sox. Likely the premier defensive shortstop of his era. Also helped bring speed back to the American League, leading the circuit in stolen bases his first nine seasons ('56-'64), a feat unmatched.

Brooks Robinson—Third Base, Baltimore Orioles. Posted his breakout year in '60, his sixth in the big leagues, by recording highs up to that point in home runs, RBI, and batting average. Also captured the first of his 16 Gold Glove awards.

Willie McCovey—First Base, San Francisco Giants. Had won the NL Rookie of the Year Award in '59 and was on his way to becoming a big slugging fan favorite in the Bay area.

Sandy Koufax—Pitcher, Los Angeles Dodgers. Just 24 years old in '60, the lefty fireballer was already in his sixth big-league season. He was still a couple of years away from his incredible five-season span of domination.

Orlando Cepeda—Outfield/First Base, San Francisco Giants. The 23-year-old native of Ponce, Puerto Rico, had captured NL Rookie of the Year honors in 1958. Was named in '60 to his second of seven All-Star teams in his 17-year career.

Bob Gibson—Pitcher, St. Louis Cardinals. The 24-year-old product of Creighton University made his debut in '59 and was being utilized as both a starter and reliever in '60. The former Harlem Globetrotter would not regret his decision to leave behind the world of exhibition basketball.

Juan Marichal—Pitcher, San Francisco Giants. The high-kicking 22-year-old Dominican gave a sign of things to come by debuting in July of '60 with a one-hit shutout. In his 11 appearances that season, all starts, he compiled a 6-2 record with a 2.66 ERA.

Bob Gibson—In his sophomore season in 1960, he was still several seasons away from his dominant years. Somewhat unconvinced of his true potential, the Cardinals offered him to the new expansion Washington Senators in mid-December of '60 in exchange for the just-drafted Bobby Shantz. Later, they would be very thankful they were turned down.

Billy Williams—Left field, Chicago Cubs. Had debuted in '59, and also played briefly for the Cubs in '60, splitting time with Houston of the American Association. At this time he reminded some of a young Hank Aaron. The first two of his 426 career home runs came this season.

Casey Stengel—Manager, New York Yankees. Celebrated his 50th anniversary in Organized Baseball in 1960, having broke in with Kankakee (Illinois) of the Northern Association in 1910. Led the Yankees to their tenth pennant in his 12 seasons as their pilot, then was promptly let go after their loss to Pittsburgh in the World Series.

Walter Alston—Manager, Los Angeles Dodgers. Skipper of the reigning World Champion Dodgers entering 1960. In his six seasons at the helm to this point, he had captured two World Series and one other NL pennant. In the off-seasons, he left behind the bright lights of L.A. to live in his hometown of Darrtown, Ohio—population: 150.

Al Lopez—Manager, Chicago White Sox. In his first nine years of managing in the majors, 1951 through '59, Lopez's teams never finished lower than second place. Won AL pennants with Cleveland in '54 and Chicago in '59.

Lou Boudreau—Manager, Chicago Cubs. The seven-time AL All-Star shortstop and 1944 batting champ was making his third managerial stop. Had previously served as player-manager for Cleveland and the Red Sox. Plucked from the Cubs broadcast booth to take over the team in May of '60.

Luke Appling—Coach, Detroit Tigers, Cleveland Indians. The premier offensive shortstop of his era, he had spent his entire 20-year playing career with the White Sox (1930-'50). Began '60 season coaching third base for the Tigers until Detroit traded manager Jimmie Dykes to Cleveland, and Dykes took Appling along with him.

Bill Dickey—Coach, New York Yankees. One of the top catchers of the 1930s, he spent his entire 17-year career in pinstripes. The former teammate of Ruth, Gehrig, and DiMaggio was part of seven World Championships during that span.

Billy Herman—Coach, Boston Red Sox. The NL's best second baseman of the 1930s was manning the third base coach's box at this time. He had managed Pittsburgh back in '47, and would go on to manage Boston from '64 to '66.

Bob Lemon—Coach, Cleveland Indians. During his 13-year pitching career (1946-'58) with Cleveland, he had seven 20-win seasons, compiling 207 lifetime victories.

Ford Frick—Commisioner, Major League Baseball. Was in his tenth year as the game's top executive after having served as NL president for 17 years.

Warren Giles—President, National League. Succeeded Frick as NL president in 1951 after a long stint as general manager of the Cincinnati Reds.

Joe Cronin—President, American League. Had been appointed to the position in 1958. Cronin rose through the ranks, compiling an impressive resume that included 19 years as player, 15 as manager, and 11 as Red Sox general manager.

George Weiss—General Manager, New York Yankees. Was Yankees G.M. during great dynasty of the late '40s and continuing throughout the 1950s. Stepped down just weeks after Pittsburgh upset Yanks in '60 Series. Named Major League Executive of the Year for 1960 by *The Sporting News*.

Stanley "Bucky" Harris—General Manager, Boston Red Sox. Had a 29-year career as a major league manager with the Senators, Tigers, Red Sox, Phillies, and Yankees. Had succeeded Cronin as Sox G.M. in '58, and would serve in that capacity until the fall of '60.

Lee MacPhail—President, General Manager, Baltimore Orioles. His father Larry, also a Hall of Famer, had been a top executive with the Reds, Dodgers, and Yankees in the 1930s and '40s. Lee had been the Yankees Director of Player Personnel in the late 1940s and '50s until taking over as Orioles G.M. Later became AL president. Was considered a favorite at this time to succeed Frick as Commissioner.

Thomas Yawkey—President, Boston Red Sox. Inherited ten million dollars at age 16 from uncle William Yawkey, who had previously been part owner of the Tigers. Notoriously generous and fatherly towards the players, his ownership of Red Sox would last 33 years. *The Sporting News* editorialized in its February 24, 1960 issue: "If baseball should ever make a place in the Hall of Fame for club owners, Yawkey should become the first to enter."

Rick Ferrell—General Manager, Vice President, Detroit Tigers. An outstanding defensive catcher and pretty fair hitter during his 18-season career from 1929 to '47. Worked in a variety of positions after retirement, including coach, scout, and executive before being appointed Tiger G.M.

Bill Veeck—President, Chicago White Sox. Previously had owned Cleveland Indians and St. Louis Browns before purchasing White Sox. Two noteworthy innovations from 1960 were putting players' names on the back of uniforms and the exploding scoreboard at Comiskey Park.

Jocko Conlan—Umpire, National League. Was now working in his 20th season as a major league umpire after a brief stint as an outfielder with the White Sox in 1934 and '35.

Al Barlick—Umpire, National League. Had begun his career as a major league umpire in 1940 at the age of 25. Retired in '72 after 33 years on the job.

Nestor Chylak—Umpire, American League. Regarded as his circuit's best arbitrator during a career that began in 1954 and concluded in 1978.

Honorable Mention: In addition to the 51 individuals listed above, the following Hall of Famers were also involved in Major League Baseball in 1960, albeit in slightly less prominent roles: Will Harridge, former AL President serving as the league's Chairman of the Board; Hank Greenberg, vice-president and treasurer of the Chicago White Sox; George Sisler, special assistant to the manager, Pittsburgh Pirates; and Cal Hubbard, former AL umpire serving as the league's supervisor of umpires.

There is the distinct possibility in the coming years that one or more of the following men could be added to the list of Hall of Famers active in 1960: continuing to be considered for election are Bill Mazeroski, Gil Hodges, Ron Santo, Minnie Minoso, and Joe Gordon, who was serving as a manager at the time.

Chapter Three

Theatres of the Game

Every summer, throngs of baseball fans travel from all over New England and beyond to make the pilgrimage to the structure that writer John Updike referred to as a "lyric little bandbox"— Fenway Park.

What attracts a large number of these spectators is not so much the team on the field, or the individual performers outfitted in "Red Sox" uniforms. For many it is the chance to be part of an event held in the same setting as those attended decades before by parents, grandparents, and in some cases great-grandparents. Built in 1912, it has become a landmark in eastern Massachusetts not terribly unlike Plymouth Rock, the U.S.S. Constitution, or the Old North Church. The faces on the field may seem to constantly change, but the "stage" for the most part has remained the same for more than three-quarters of a century.

A major league baseball game is very much an event in the same way that a symphony, an opera, a play, a ballet, or a concert is. Aficionados and enthusiasts purchase a ticket, find their way to their seats, and observe professionals performing their craft. Be it Radio City Music Hall, Ford Theatre, The Grand Ole Opry, or Wrigley

Field, the "theatre" itself is often as memorable as the event taking place.

There were 16 such theatres showcasing major league baseball in the spring and summer of 1960. In approximate order of their stature within the history of the game, they were:

American League

Yankee Stadium, New York—Without question the most hallowed of all parks in which the game has been played. When the Yankees hosted the Pittsburgh Pirates in the 1960 World Series, it marked the 23rd Fall Classic that had taken place there since it was built 37 years earlier. The 1939 All-Star Game, as well as the second Midsummer Classic of '60 had also been held there to that point. Some of baseball's most historic and solemn occasions had taken place there, including "Lou Gehrig Day" in 1939; Babe Ruth's farewell appearance two months prior to his death in '48; and Babe's record-breaking 60th homer on September 30, 1927.

Fenway Park, Boston—Home to four world championship teams in its first seven seasons (1912, '15, '16, '18), but still seeking its fifth as the new century arrives. Among the legendary figures to call Fenway home have been Tris Speaker, a young Babe Ruth, Lefty Grove, Jimmie Foxx, Ted Williams, and Carl Yastrzemski. The park itself underwent major reconstruction in 1934 after being purchased by Tom Yawkey the year before.

Tiger Stadium, Detroit—Also known as "Briggs Stadium". Having opened for business on the same day as Fenway Park back in 1912, the old ballyard was in its 49th summer in 1960. Had hosted the World Series in '34, '35, '40, and '45, and All-Star games in 1941 and '51.

Fenway Park—The site of many historic baseball happenings, including Ted Williams' memorable final major league game. (Courtesy, Sports Museum of New England)

Comiskey Park, Chicago—Occupying a site that was formerly a city dump, the park, built in 1910, was the oldest in the AL at this time. The first All-Star Game took place here in 1933, along with the 1950 game. Innovative team owner Bill Veeck had the first-ever exploding scoreboard installed in 1960.

Griffith Stadium, Washington D.C.—Made its debut just nine months after Comiskey Park, April, 1911. Smallest seating capacity in majors in '60 at 28,669. Nineteen sixty would be the final season the original Senators used the park before departing to Minnesota.

Municipal Stadium, Cleveland—The park with the AL's largest seating capacity at 78,811 was built in the early 1930s in hopes of attracting the '32 Olympics, which never came. Host to the '48 World Series and '35 and '48 All-Star games.

Memorial Stadium, Baltimore—Originally built in 1932, the park had been remodeled and was renamed when the St. Louis Browns transferred to Baltimore before the 1954 season.

Municipal Stadium, Kansas City—Served as the home field for the Negro League Kansas City Monarchs from 1923 to 1950. Became the home of the Athletics after they moved from Philadelphia before the 1955 season.

National League

Wrigley Field, Chicago—Originally built in 1914 to house Chicago's Federal League team, the Cubs moved in two years later after that circuit died. Site of Babe Ruth's famous and controversial "called shot" in the 1932 World Series. The ivy on the outfield wall was planted by Bill Veeck in 1937.

Forbes Field, Pittsburgh—Home of the Pirates since 1909, an 18-foot bronze statue of all-time great shortstop Honus Wagner stood behind the left field wall. Was the site of two very famous home runs—Babe Ruth's final in the majors, number 714, and Bill Mazeroski's classic blast to win the '60 Series.

Crosley Field, Cincinnati—Opened in 1912, just eight days before Fenway and Tiger Stadium. Had been the scene of the first night game in major league history on May 24, 1935. Saw world series action in the infamous "Black Sox" series of 1919, and versus Detroit in 1940. NL's smallest seating capacity in '60 at 30,328.

Connie Mack Stadium, Philadelphia—Also known as Shibe Park, the Phillies had shared this park with the Athletics from 1938 through 1954. In '56, the outfield scoreboard from Yankee Stadium was relocated here in right center field. Hosted All-Star games in 1943 and '52.

Forbes Field—The park that served the Pittsburgh Pirates for 62 seasons (1909-1970). (National Baseball Library)

Sportsman's Park, St. Louis—Cardinals were co-tenants at this park with the St. Louis Browns from 1920 through 1953. Site of the inter-city World Series between the two teams in 1944. Also the site of Bill Veeck's publicity stunt of sending 3'7" Eddie Gaedel up to pinch-hit on August 19, 1953.

Candlestick Park, San Francisco—Brand new in 1960, its first major league action came on Opening Day, April 12. Players immediately began to complain about the cold and winds blowing in from left field. No telling how many home runs Willie Mays would ultimately lose to these winds.

Candlestick Park, San Francisco, which would be the home park of four future Hall of Famers in 1960—Willie Mays, Orlando Cepeda, Willie McCovey, and rookie Juan Marichal. This photo was taken at the park's inaugural game on April 12, 1960. (National Baseball Library)

County Stadium, Milwaukee—Became the Braves' new park upon their arrival from Boston in the Spring of 1953. Had hosted the Fall Classics in '57 and '58, and the Midsummer Classic in 1955.

Los Angeles Memorial Coliseum—Had been the Dodgers' home since their shocking move from Brooklyn after the '57 season. The college football stadium had, by far, the largest seating capacity in the majors in '60 at 94,600. Because of its odd shape, the left field foul pole was just 251 feet from home. A 40-foot screen in left prevented homers from being too easily attained.

Chapter Four

Play Ball! Glimpses From Opening Week

Due to a scheduling quirk, the National League opened its 1960 season a week before the American League did. This was the first time they did not open simultaneously since 1902, before the two circuits had agreed to peacefully coexist. Many were highly critical of the AL's decision to allow the NL to spend a week alone in the spotlight while they were still engaged in meaningless exhibition games, and several AL executives vowed it wouldn't happen again.

For the San Francisco Giants, April 12 was much more than just a game against the St. Louis Cardinals on the first day of the new season. It was the official unveiling of their $15 million, just-completed 43,765 seat stadium and all the pomp and ceremony that went with it. A formal pre-game dedication took place at home plate at which vice-president and California native Richard Nixon and the state's governor, Pat Brown, spoke.

Nixon told the crowd, "San Francisco can say that this is the finest ballpark in the country. It's a magnificent stadium in which to have a World Series." The governor added, "San Francisco has always been a city of giants. Now we have a home for them." Paying homage to the franchise's great past, the widow of John McGraw,

Willie Mays and vice-president Richard Nixon sharing a laugh before the start of the Opening Day game at the brand new Candlestick Park. (National Baseball Library)

the legendary manager from the early part of the century, was introduced to the crowd. Nixon, who threw out the first pitch, also took the time to pose for photographs with such diamond luminaries as Stan Musial and Ty Cobb.

The inaugural crowd of 42,269 was treated to a stellar performance by veteran ace Sam Jones, who christened the new park with a three-hit complete-game 3-1 win over Musial's Cardinals. Orlando Cepeda was the offensive star, driving in all of the Giants' three runs with a triple and a single. The following day, San Francisco's Mike McCormick matched Jones' feat with a three-hit victory of his own. He actually had a no-hitter going until Musial led off the eighth with a single to left field on a two- and-two count. This marked the third time in the past year that Musial had broken up a no-hitter in the late innings of a game.

Candlestick Park was barely a week old when many were calling for the outfield fences to be moved in. The power alley in right center field measured 397 feet, and stiff winds blew from left straight across the field to right. Willie Mays stated, "I'll hit only a few homers, and they'll want me to take a [pay] cut." Only 80 home runs would be hit there altogether in 1960, the fewest hit in any major league park that season.

A throng of 67,550, a new record for a night game, were present at the Los Angeles Coliseum on April 12 for the Dodgers' opener against the Cubs. After NL president Warren Giles tossed out the first pitch, Dodger ace Don Drysdale went to work and hurled 11 strong innings, striking out 14. Pinch-hitter Chuck Essegian was sent up to bat for Drysdale in the bottom of the eleventh with the score knotted at two. Essegian, who barely survived the final cut in Spring Training, had slugged two pinch-hit home runs in the previous fall's World Series. Here in his first at-bat of 1960, he did the same, sending the Dodgers home with a 3-2 win.

An unusual situation transpired with the Philadelphia Phillies just after Opening Day. The team had traveled to Cincinnati to kick the season off with one game against the Reds and were pummeled 9-4. The following day with no game scheduled, the Phillies were back home and held a noontime workout at Connie Mack Stadium. Afterward, manager Eddie Sawyer contacted team general manager John Quinn and indicated that he was considering resigning after just one game. Phils owner Bob Carpenter then had several phone conversations with Sawyer that evening and finally at 3 a.m. accepted his resignation. Quinn then contacted Red Sox general manager Bucky Harris for permission to discuss the job with Gene Mauch, manager of Boston's top farm team in Minneapolis. Permission was granted, and Mauch was hired, beginning an extremely noteworthy managerial career that lasted 26 seasons. Regarding his untimely departure, Sawyer said, "Things had been building up for several weeks. There wasn't any one thing, just a lot of things." Though he was interested in remaining in the game in some capacity, he stated, "I never want to manage a major league club again."

The Giants continued to benefit from impressive performances from their pitching staff. Sam Jones followed up his Opening Day three-hitter with a one-hitter against Chicago in his second start on Saturday, April 16. The Cubs' lone hit came with two outs in the eighth inning as Walt Moryn connected for a pinch-hit solo homer. Jones, who became the first black pitcher in major league history to toss a no-hitter back in 1955, settled for the one-hit 2-1 win. The next day, Easter Sunday, two noteworthy events occurred in the National League. Just before the Dodgers were to host St. Louis, the NL and World Championship banners were raised at the Coliseum. With NL president Warren Giles looking on, Commissioner Ford Frick presented the Dodger players with their World Series rings. Around this same time at Connie Mack Stadium, Braves third baseman Eddie Mathews was slugging his 300th career home run off Robin Roberts. At the age of 28 years, 6 months, and 4 days, Mathews was the second youngest ever to reach the figure, behind only slugger Jimmie Foxx at 27 years, 10 months, and 23 days.

It was the following day, April 18 that the American League finally joined the NL by kicking off its regular season. The place was the nation's capital, and 28,237 turned out for what would be the final Opening Day for the original Washington Senators franchise. The festivities the following year would take place in Bloomington, Minnesota.

On this Monday in 1960, the Senators hosted the Boston Red Sox and Ted Williams. President Dwight Eisenhower interrupted a golf vacation in Augusta, Georgia, to perform the duty of throwing out the first ball at the Senators' opener for the final time. The tradition of the president engaging in that ceremony at the Senators' opener began 50 years before, when William Howard Taft did so on April 14, 1910. Vice president Nixon, seated beside Eisenhower, was running for president at this time and may well have envisioned this duty belonging to him the next year. Speaking at a dinner a week before, Nixon told the crowd, "Washington has about as much chance to win the American League pennant as I have to win the 'Democratic' nomination for president."

Williams came up to bat to lead off the second inning and deposited a 450-foot home run into the center field bleachers for a 1-0 lead. The president tipped his hat to Ted as he crossed home plate. That was the extent of the Red Sox offense as Washington dominated, winning by a score of 10-1. The Senators' young Cuban right handed hurler Camilo Pascual was phenomenal, allowing only three hits and striking out a whopping 15 batters. Ted lavished praise on the youngster, saying after the game, "Nobody in this league can compare with that pitcher. He showed me a better fastball and a better curve than I've seen one pitcher put together in this league." There were others who also regarded Pascual as the best in the AL at this time.

The day after the Red Sox' one-game series opener in Washington, they were back in Boston for their home opener against the Yankees. This marked the official Yankee debut for young Roger Maris, and he gave a sign of things to come with his performance.

U.S. president Dwight Eisenhower performed the duty of throwing out the first pitch on Opening Day for the final time on April 18, 1960.

After spending virtually the entire spring playing left field, Maris now found himself in right field to stay. He was utilized in the lead off spot in the order, and he turned in a fine four-for-five day, with two home runs, a double, a single, and four RBI in New York's 8-4 win at Fenway Park.

Another two-home run day was posted on this Opening Day by Minnie Minoso in his return to the White Sox, who were hosting the Athletics. He had connected for a grand slam early in the game, and later belted a solo homer in the ninth to give Chicago the victory in the 10-9 slugfest. After the game, Minoso recalled his memorable first game over with the White Sox on April 30, 1951, in which he homered in his first at-bat.

In the wake of the historic Colavito/Kuenn trade, the two teams would coincidentally open up against each other in Cleveland on April 19. The match-up created such excitement that more than 19,000 walk-up tickets were sold. The Tigers came out on top this time in a marathon 15-inning affair by a tally of 4-2. Colavito did not factor in the win, going 0-for-six with four strikeouts, while Kuenn had two hits and played well in the field. Kuenn, however, pulled a muscle in his leg and was unable to play the next day, while Rocky hit a three-run homer to help Detroit win 6-4. Two days later, the Tigers held their home opener at Briggs Stadium versus Chicago, and Colavito won the crowd over early by socking a home run in his first at-bat. The Tigers announced during this game that as of October 2, the final day of the season, Briggs Stadium would officially become known as "Tiger Stadium". The Detroit opener on April 22 also bore witness to a baseball first—the Chicago White Sox officially unveiled their new road uniforms with the players' names on the back. White Sox players were not too pleased with

Nellie Fox's 1960 Chicago White Sox road jersey, which was the first uniform to feature players' names on the back. (Courtesy, National Baseball Hall of Fame and Museum)

Bill Veeck's innovation, citing increased recognizability by the fans. One player sniped , "All we really need now are our telephone numbers on our uniforms, and we'll have as much privacy as goldfish."

While Detroit was hosting its 1960 inaugural, AL president Joe Cronin was handling the duty of throwing out the first pitch at the Yankees home opener. New York topped Baltimore 5-0 on a combined effort from Whitey Ford and Ralph Terry. Mickey Mantle hit a home run, and also reached a milestone—his 1,000th career run scored. The Yankees were now on their way to a milestone as well: the tenth and final pennant of the Stengel era.

Chapter Five

The Kid's Swan Song

As of early January 1960, Ted Williams' status as an active player was very much up in the air. Rumors were flying in the Boston daily papers as to the manner in which he would be spending the upcoming season. One said Ted was offered a contract as a broadcaster for Red Sox games on local television. Another had owner Tom Yawkey paying Ted his salary while he devoted himself to his fishing tackle business, then returning in 1961 as a color commentator on Sox games.

Williams had received his contract for 1960 in the mail by mid-January and would be traveling from his home in Florida to discuss it with Boston general manager Bucky Harris the following week. It was at this time that Red Sox trainer Jack Fadden called Ted and convinced him that he could play despite his aches and pains. It was a variety of ailments, including a bad back, a bad leg, and a nagging neck injury that caused him to appear in only 103 games in 1959.

Arriving in Boston on January 22 he told the media, "If I still have this pain in my neck, I won't play." He was given a complete three-hour physical exam the following day at the renowned

Lahey Clinic, located north of Boston and received a clean bill of health, along with exercises to help his neck. On the morning of January 25 at 8:45, he slipped into Fenway Park's executive offices to meet with Harris. With no fanfare, no reporters, and no cameras, Williams unceremoniously put his name on the dotted line for the final time and quietly slipped out to get a haircut around the corner in Kenmore Square. His signing became even more important to the Red Sox the following day when the team learned that All-Star outfielder Jackie Jensen was retiring prematurely. As for why Williams would return for another season at the age of 41 despite his physical woes, he would later cite four main reasons at a press gathering in Baltimore in April. He was embarrassed about the season he had in 1959, in which he hit well below .300 for the first time in his career; he still felt his hitting could help the Red Sox; he had his sights set on attaining the milestone of 500 home runs, along with 2,000 career bases on balls, achieved by only Babe Ruth; and he also felt he was not in a financial position to walk away from the money he could still earn in the game.

The Red Sox training camp of 1960 officially opened in Scottsdale, Arizona on February 25. One Boston newspaper referred back to Ted's first camp with the team in 1938 in Sarasota, Florida, where upon his arrival, the brash 19-year-old announced, "Wait until (Jimmie) Foxx and (Joe) Cronin see me hit."

Ted arrived in Scottsdale for his final major league Spring Training on March 1 after a harrowing 14-hour flight from Miami. Still complaining of a sore neck, he said he wasn't sure he would be able to play. He was also sporting a special brace to alleviate his aching back. On March 2, Manager Jurges announced that Williams would also take on the duties of an assistant batting coach during camp. He would be tutoring a few of the younger players, and it was believed that young Carl Yastrzemski was to be one of his first pupils. When he witnessed the 20-year-old Yaz swing that spring, he said, "I'm not going to try to teach that boy anything. He is a natural." Ted took batting practice and showed no apparent

Ted Williams displaying his classic swing in September of 1960.

effects from his troublesome neck. Two teammates were razzing him a bit, even going so far as to place wagers on his performance. He responded by crushing two home runs over the right-field fence.

While Bostonians were digging out from a foot and a half of snow, a *Boston Globe* sportswriter predicted for his readers on March 4 that Ted's bad neck has caused him to alter his stance, and he would never again be a great hitter as a result. Jurges was taking a different approach with Williams this spring by planning to play him into shape, rather than allowing him to set his own conditioning program. Ted broke with personal tradition by playing in all six innings of the team's first intra-squad game on March 6. In the 80-degree heat, he made a long run to deep center field to make a nice catch. In another intra-squad contest on March 9 he slugged a 380-foot home run.

With Ty Cobb in attendance, Ted appeared in the Sox' first official Spring Training game on March 11 versus the Chicago Cubs. The teams met again the next day also, and in the two games Ted walked twice, struck out once, and was hit by a pitch. On March 14, general manager Harris described Ted's first two weeks as quite pleasing. Williams himself said at this time, "I'm coming along, but I'm not completely satisfied. I find that I can't push my conditioning like I used to. But I do know that my legs are coming along in good shape."

Over the next couple of weeks, however, frustration began to set in for Ted. Though he had been playing fairly regularly, hits weren't coming very frequently, and when they did, they came in the form of singles. After working out hard on the morning of March 25, he reportedly told a teammate, "This is it." In a *Boston Herald* column two days later, Ed Costello wrote, "Now it appears that Ted Williams is on the verge of giving up the fight to remain an active player after 20 years as a member of the Red Sox." Costello had observed that Williams was a little plumper around the midsection than when he arrived, and that Ted himself appeared disgusted over his physical condition. Others observed that he just didn't have the same zip in the past ten days or so.

He plodded along, when on March 29 he left camp after receiving word that his 39-year-old brother Danny passed away in San Diego. Ted immediately departed for his hometown to attend the funeral. It was at this time that the Red Sox turned down a proposed deal with the Dodgers for Williams. L.A. general manager Buzzie Bavasi felt he "would be a tremendous draw even if he only sat on the bench."

After returning to training camp on April 1, talk seemed to subside regarding Ted's imminent retirement as he continued to work toward Opening Day. The Red Sox played the Cardinals in Scottsdale on April 6, and noted sports columnist Bud Collins referred to the Musial versus Williams matchup as an "antique show". The two legends acquitted themselves well, with Ted stroking two singles and Musial smacking a three-run homer to help win the 13-10 game.

Williams had two more hits the following day against the Giants in Phoenix. Afterwards, Red Sox trainer Fadden said, "If Ted could play the regular season in Arizona, he'd go on indefinitely. His neck hasn't bothered him. The heat is excellent for him." Unfortunately, this was to be their last spring game in Arizona as they set out for a week and a half tour leading up to Opening Day. The Red Sox engaged in exhibitions in such locales as New Orleans, St. Petersburg, Sarasota, and Daytona Beach, and manager Jurges seemed pleased with Ted's progress. At this time, he remarked, "I hope he gets those eight homers to reach 500 and a lot more, but I can't let him stay in there just for the sake of reaching a personal goal unless he's really hitting." Around the same time, Ted told noted New York baseball writer Dan Daniel, "I would like to get to the 500 level, but I am not going to hang on as a .220 hitter."

The Red Sox concluded their 1960 exhibition season with two games against the Yankees in the Bronx on April 16 and 17.

With temperatures in the low fifties, Ted skipped the first game, as Jurges didn't want him to risk injury. He singled in his only at-bat in the finale, and though he had hit .333 for the spring, uncharacteristically only two of his 15 hits were for extra bases.

Ted's 19th and final major league season officially began at Griffith Stadium in Washington on Monday, April 18. The pregame festivities included vice-president Nixon walking out to the flagpole and helping to raise Old Glory. Ted's first at-bat came with one out in the second inning, and he typically worked the count to three and two. He then wasted no time in his march toward 500 home runs by rocketing a 420-foot blast into the bleachers for career number 493, tying him for fourth on the all-time list with Lou Gehrig. Ted had made his major league debut against Gehrig and the Yankees on April 20, 1939, which was Opening Day of Gehrig's ill-fated final season.

After the one-game series in Washington to open the season, the Red Sox were back in Boston for the Fenway Park opener the following day, April 19. An overflow crowd of 35,162 jammed into the Beantown ball yard on Patriot's Day to see the archrival Yankees help kick off the local baseball season. *New York Times* sportswriter Arthur Daley wrote that Ted arrived for the opener, "with joy in his heart and a smile on his lips." Williams put a lot of smiles on a lot of lips in the eighth inning with a home run into the right field stands. Roger Maris raced over, but the ball beat him there as the fans erupted with a tremendous ovation. Gehrig's old team had allowed Ted to move past him for sole possession of the number-four rank on the homer list with his 494th. He also looked good out in left field when he played a Gil McDougald drive off the wall perfectly and held him to a single. After the game, Ted cautioned, "I'm on a day-to-day basis and just hope to get through the season." Unfortunately, he had a very good reason for making this statement. When he hit his home run, he initially didn't think it went out and started to dig for a double, pulling a muscle in his left leg.

He sat out the next day's game, and was primarily relegated to pinch-hitting duty for the next few weeks.

During the Red Sox-Yankees series, Casey Stengel recalled being impressed with a young Ted Williams way back in 1937 when he was doing a bit of scouting for the old Boston Braves. Stengel advised the Braves to sign him at that time; however, when a Braves representative went to look at him, he ended up signing one of Ted's San Diego teammates. It seems that San Diego felt obligated to deal with the Red Sox regarding Ted due to a previous arrangement. It is interesting to ponder the idea of Ted beginning his major league career with Boston's National League team rather than with the Red Sox. As for Stengel, Williams said of him in late April of 1960, "He's contributed more to baseball than anyone in the game today." Stengel was also quoted at this time in the current issue of *Sports Illustrated*, saying, "Williams looks so much better up at the plate than most everybody else in the league that all the pitchers better forget how old he is and be careful."

Also in late April, rumors began to surface that Ted would take over as the Red Sox manager after he quit playing. He quickly squelched the rumors, and called managing "one of the lousiest jobs there is."

Injuries were crippling the Red Sox in early May, and it wasn't until the 21st of the month in Cleveland that Ted made his return to the starting line-up. The team was struggling terribly, and trouble loomed for manager Jurges, who was under extreme stress at this time. The situation came to a head after a tough loss on June 7, and the team announced that Jurges would be taking a leave of absence due to ill health. Sox coach Del Baker took the team over temporarily, and some members of the Boston press were encouraging Ted to take the managerial reins, of which he wanted no part. The Red Sox made it official on June 10 that Jurges would not be returning to the helm, and two days later announced the hiring of Mike Higgins, who had been fired from the position in July of 1959.

Taking over the Red Sox on June 12 of '60, Higgins found the team mired in last place with a record of 17 and 32.

By mid-June, Williams was creeping up on the coveted 500-home run plateau. On June 16 at Briggs Stadium in Detroit, a homer haven for Williams over the years, he connected for number 499. Though the Red Sox eventually lost the game 6-5, Ted's ninth-inning upper-deck homer off Hank Aguirre tied the score at 5-5.

It was the following night, June 17, as the team had continued on their road trip to Cleveland that the historic blow was struck. It was a misty, chilly Friday evening, with only 9,765 Indians fans scattered around massive Municipal Stadium. In his second at-bat of the game facing Wynn Hawkins in the third inning, he drove the ball, a slider, into a strong wind over the left field wall. Cleveland writer Hal Lebovitz wrote that Ted was " . . . as frisky as a rookie as he dashed around the bases."

As he crossed home plate, Ted was mobbed by his team-mates, and manager Higgins would later say that although Williams didn't say much, it was obvious he was overjoyed. Two weeks earlier, Ted had a bad cold, was slumping at bat, and was considering retirement. Now he was basking in the glow of one of the biggest highlights of his long career. AL president Joe Cronin, who was Williams' first manager back in 1939 and had witnessed his first major league home run off Philadelphia's Luther Thomas happened to be on hand for the milestone. Cronin was at the game for the presentation of Cleveland's Harvey Kuenn's batting title award for 1959. The historic ball was retrieved by an usher and handed over to the Red Sox bullpen, and later Ted said he would donate it to the Jimmy Fund Cancer charity to be auctioned off to the highest bidder.

Williams also took the time to reflect back to 1940 when his teammate, legendary slugger Jimmie Foxx, hit his 500th career homer. Just after Ted reached the milestone, the 50-year old Foxx, speaking from the Jimmie Foxx Restaurant in Galesburg, Illinois, recalled a conversation the two men had two years prior. He stated that Williams was on the verge of retiring, but he convinced him to continue his pursuit of 500 home runs. Ted also told the press after the game that he was setting his sights on 512 home runs next—a reference to passing former Giants slugger Mel Ott, who was third on the all-time list with 511. He also made clear his intention to continue playing just as long as management wanted him around. As long as he was hitting home runs at the clip he had been maintaining recently, there was no reason not to want him around. Two days after his 500th, which helped beat Cleveland 3-1, he drilled a three-run shot that was his sixth in his previous eight games. On June 29 his 11th home run of the month helped the Red Sox beat Detroit 4-2 in Boston.

In early July, the results of All-Star voting—with the teams being selected by fellow players—were announced. Ted was among those voted to the AL squad, and would be appearing on the mid-summer classic team for the 16th time. He was undoubtedly a legend even amongst his peers, and later that summer *The Sporting News* editorialized , "Ted has the universal respect of all players, teammates and opponents, as well as umpires. Their affection for him is unbounded."

Three days before the first of the two All-Star games, Williams recorded another impressive statistical milestone. Driving in his 1,800th career run on July 10 versus the Yankees at Boston, he joined a club that included only six truly upper-echelon hitters—Al Simmons, Ott, Foxx, Ty Cobb, Lou Gehrig, and Babe Ruth.

Ted took a league-leading .341 batting average into the All-Star break. In the first match-up of the game's top stars in Kansas City on July 13, he pinch-hit in the second inning and grounded out. Two days later, the exhibition moved on to New York's Yankee Stadium, and Ted singled in his only at-bat, pinch-hitting for Minnie Minoso. This now closed the book on his All-Star game statistics. In 45 at-bats against the NL's best, he was 14 for 45 (.311) with four home runs and 12 RBI.

At his final midsummer classic appearance, Williams told a reporter, "I've been feeling real good, and that's the reason I've been hitting. But I'm not kidding myself that this can go on indefinitely. I have to figure that this is my last season." Shortly after the second half of the season resumed, Ted continued his climb up the home run ladder. By the end of July, he was one round-tripper shy of Ott's National League record of 511. A few days later, speaking at a Jimmy Fund luncheon in Boston, Ted again hinted strongly at retirement after this season.

After going a week-and-a-half without homering, Williams finally caught up with Ott, pounding out number 511 on August 9 in Cleveland. He then quickly put Ott behind him by slugging two more against the Indians the following day. In telling reporters of his intention to make this his last season he stated, "I want to quit with a good year, and this is it." Some of his teammates couldn't understand why, as they felt he was hitting the ball as well as he ever had. Essentially, Ted had accomplished what he had set out to do by atoning for his miserable 1959 season, and attaining the major milestones. In mid-August, a major honor was bestowed upon him as *The Sporting News* named him the "Player of the Decade" for the 1950s. While basking in this distinction, Williams had what was likely his most spectacular game of the season on August 20. That day he slugged two three-run homers versus the Orioles in the 8-6 Boston victory, and also drew his 2,000th career walk, moving him behind only Ruth in that category.

Six days later, Ted suffered a slight shoulder injury banging into Fenway's left-field wall attempting to make a catch off the bat of Chicago's Roy Sievers. He missed three games and returned against the Tigers on August 30, his 42nd birthday. While he stated that all he wanted for his birthday was contributions to the Jimmy Fund, he may well have wished for a few more Red Sox victories. The team was heading into the month of September with a 55-71 record, mired in seventh place. While the team wasn't racking up many victories, Ted was continuing to rack up homers. His 25th of the season on September 2 was an illustration of just how long he had been on the major league scene. After connecting that day off Washington's Don Lee, he said he remembered hitting a couple off Don's father Thornton, who pitched for Chicago back in the late 1930s and '40s.

One of Williams' most famous home runs came in the All-Star game of 1941 at Tiger Stadium. A total of 54 of his career homers had come in Detroit—more than any other ballpark he had visited. On September 7, during what would be his last series played there, the Tigers held "Ted Williams Night" to honor him, which featured a pre-game ceremony. He was quoted as saying that if he had to play for any other team in baseball, he would have enjoyed playing for Detroit. During the game, he reminded the fans with his bat that he still played for Boston, as his double and single drove in two runs in their 5-4 victory over the Tigers.

Ted's next-to-last career homer, number 520, was a two-run shot in Washington that beat the Senators 2-1 on September 17. Three days later in Baltimore, he fouled a pitch off his right ankle in the first inning, severely bruising it. He limped around for a minute or two, and Higgins then replaced him with pinch-hitter Carroll Hardy. Although there was considerable swelling, X-rays proved negative. It was around this same time that Ted's two-story home in the Florida Keys was destroyed by Hurricane Donna. It was speculated initially that the loss might change his retirement plans.

Ted was able to return to the line-up for the three-game series versus the Yankees in Boston beginning on September 23. After the first game, the *Boston Herald's* Ralph Wheeler wrote that Ted "pranced around like a colt despite his ankle injury of earlier this week." Williams hit safely in each game, going five for 11, but the Yankees swept as the victory in the final game on the 25th officially captured the AL pennant. However, the New York clinching was upstaged by Tom Yawkey's press conference immediately following the game. The Red Sox owner made official what most suspected; Ted Williams' storied baseball playing career was over after the 1960 season. Ted himself simply added, "There'll be no more playing. That's right. This is the last year."

As the country was still buzzing over the first Kennedy/Nixon presidential debate, Baltimore came to Boston for a two-game series that would close out the Red Sox season at home. Boston was then scheduled to travel to New York for the final three games of the year. Though it was not learned until later, Ted had apparently decided before the final Baltimore game on September 28 that it would be his last appearance. It was a Wednesday afternoon, a day with a threat of rain and fog that hung heavily in the air, and only 10,454 patrons in Fenway's stands. A 15-minute pregame ceremony to honor Ted was held at home plate, with the city, state, and Chamber of Commerce all paying tribute. He was presented with many gifts, including a $4,000 check for the Jimmy Fund, and though he appeared a bit fidgety, he calmed down when he stepped up to the microphone. He told the crowd, "I'm convinced I quit at the right time. There's nothing more I can do. If I were asked where I would like to have played, I would have to say Boston. It has the greatest owner in baseball and the greatest fans in America."

In the first inning of his historic farewell game, he drew a walk from starter Steve Barber, scoring a few plays later on a sacrifice fly. In the third inning, just before he flied to deep center field, it was announced to the crowd that Ted's famous uniform number nine would now be officially retired for all time by the Red Sox. He would be the first Boston player to receive such an honor. Then in the fifth he hit a blast to deep right-center field. It got caught up in the heavy air and wind and was hauled in right against the Oriole bullpen. As Williams approached home plate in the eighth inning, the crowd let loose with the biggest ovation yet, figuring that this could be the last time they would witness his legendary swing. He let Fisher's first delivery go by for ball one, then swung and missed the second pitch to even the count.

This set the stage for truly one of the most splendid moments in his long and fabled tenure. Williams drilled the next offering, a fastball, just to the right of center field; a Herculean blast that fought through the elements, carried over the Red Sox bullpen, and caromed off the roof of the bullpen bench. The crowd erupted in a frenzy as he raced around the bases, quickly disappearing into the Boston dugout. The crowd pleaded for him to step out for a curtain call; his teammates begged him to do the same; and even homeplate umpire Ed Hurley held up the game, but Ted simply pulled on his warm-up jacket and remained seated.

As for Oriole pitcher Fisher, it is interesting that when he was born on March 4, 1939, Ted was just completing the first week of training camp back in his rookie season. It is also worth noting that the only other significant baseball event that Fisher was involved in was surrendering Roger Maris's 60th home run almost

Ted Williams—Saying farewell to the fans at Fenway Park for the final time on September 28, 1960. The relationship he had with fans, and especially reporters was a stormy one over his 19-season career. (Courtesy, Sports Museum of New England)

exactly a year after Williams' final homer.

After Ted's career finale, which Boston won 5-4, he told reporters "That's the end. There's nothing more I can do. I was gunning for that big one," he admitted. "I wanted badly for it to wind up that way." He then revealed his plans to attend the World Series, then return to Florida to begin the process of having his home rebuilt. He would reportedly then be off to Spain to attend the bullfights. All in all, he had put together a truly remarkable season at 42 years old; 29 home runs, a .316 batting average, and 72 RBI in only 310 at-bats. In particular, his home run percentage of 9.4 was the highest of his career in any season in which he had at least 100 at-bats. Unfortunately, the Red Sox suffered through their worst season record-wise since Tom Yawkey had bought the team back in 1933.

After 19 big-league seasons, he was leaving behind a statistical legacy to place him among the game's most elite, not to mention the lingering speculation as to just how much more impressive it may have looked without having missed four-and-a half prime seasons to two stints in the military. And now, at the end of September of 1960, Williams stood less than six years away from a date with a podium in Cooperstown, New York.

Chapter Six

Dominican Dandy's Dazzling Debut

On July 9, 1960, a 21-year-old pitcher from the Dominican Republic pitched a three-hit shutout for Tacoma of the Pacific Coast League. His won-loss record now stood at 11 and 5, and he reigned as his league's leader in strikeouts. Immediately after the impressive victory in Sacramento, his manager Red Davis informed him that he was being called up to the team's major league affiliate, the San Francisco Giants. He had just pitched his final minor league game.

Ten days later, Juan Antonio Marichal made an extremely memorable major league debut, giving a good indication of things to come in the process. When the final out was recorded on that Tuesday evening, young Marichal had allowed just one eighth-inning single in the 2-0 complete game over Philadelphia at Candlestick Park.

Juan Marichal made an auspicious major league debut and gave a sign of things to come, throwing a one-hitter on July 19, 1960.

Mixing fastballs and curves with a very effective change up, young Marichal retired the first 19 Phillies he faced. Then with one out in the seventh inning, second baseman Tony Taylor hit a grounder that shortstop Eddie Bressoud bobbled for an error. Later, with two out in the eighth and the no-hitter still intact, Phils manager Gene Mauch sent Clay Dalrymple up to pinch-hit for catcher Cal Neeman. On Marichal's first delivery to Dalrymple, he singled sharply to center field for what would be the Phillies' only safety. Giants outfielder Willie Kirkland and third baseman Jim Davenport each had RBI singles in the 2-0 victory.

For the record, no pitcher in the 20th Century made his major league debut with a no-hitter. In an odd coincidence however, fellow Latin Pedro Ramos pitched a one-hitter for Washington on the same day as Marichal's, having his gem broken up in the eighth inning also. Marichal would only issue one walk in his contest while racking up an impressive 12 strikeouts. He followed up his terrific debut with another very fine outing four days later against Pittsburgh. On that day, July 23, Marichal tossed a four-hitter for the second of his 243 career wins. He would finally get his no-hitter three years later versus the Houston Colt .45's on June 15, 1963.

Marichal could likely go down as one of the all-time bargains, as the Giants paid only $500 to sign him before the 1958 season. When Marichal came to camp with the team that spring, former Giants ace Carl Hubbell, now head of the team's farm system, said he was amazed at his control and the fact that he needed virtually no coaching. Upon the young pitcher's arrival with San Francisco in July of '60, Tom Sheehan said, "He has more pitching sense than anybody I've seen around here."

The "Dominican Dandy" was elected to the Baseball Hall of Fame in 1983 and still owns the distinction of having the best career strikeout-to-walk ratio among all enshrined pitchers. To say that the $500 the Giants paid for him back in 1958 was a bargain is certainly an understatement.

Chapter Seven

Home Runs—Milestones and a Derby

Though it generally may not be thought of as such, 1960 could possibly be regarded in its own right as the "year of the home run". Upon close inspection, it seems that an inordinate amount of personal milestone homers were slugged throughout the campaign.

Most players will readily recall such achievements—their first home run; their 100th; their 300th, etc., with the actual ball becoming a treasured part of their personal memorabilia. From the memorable first to the magical and extremely exclusive 500th, the following players reached so-called milestone home run figures during the 1960 season:

#1

Young Cubs Billy Williams, a left fielder who went on to the Hall of Fame, and likely future Hall of Famer Ron Santo both connected for career homer number one. For Williams it was the first of 426. Third baseman Santo would total 342.

#100

Bill "Moose" Skowron, Yankee first baseman, slugged his 100th during this campaign. Skowron was the starting first baseman on eight Yankee pennant winners, then moved on to the Dodgers in '63 and immediately won a World Series there.

#150

Right fielders Frank Robinson and Rocky Colavito were fellow rookies back in 1956 with the Ohio rival Reds and Indians. Each reached their 150th round-tripper this season.

#200

Milwaukee Braves teammates Hank Aaron and Joe Adcock each achieved home run number 200 this season. The pair combined for a career total of 1,091 homers. When Adcock retired after the 1967 season, his 336 ranked 20th on the all-time list.

A young Hank Aaron posing with the tool of his trade. He told a reporter in the summer of 1960, "I'm no home-run hitter." (National Baseball Library)

#225

Slugging first baseman Roy Sievers' 10th of '60 was career number 225. He had led the AL with 42 homers in '57 with Washington. Sievers concluded in 1965 with 318 total. Richard Nixon's favorite ballplayer in the late 1950s, Sievers was like a real life Joe Hardy of "Damn Yankees"—a Washington Senator born in Hannibal, Missouri.

#250

Cubs shortstop Ernie Banks was compiling home run numbers unheard of for his position. On June 30 versus the Braves at Wrigley Field, he connected for his 250th career blast.

#275

No list of noteworthy home run hitters from this period would be complete without the name of Willie Mays, whose 25th homer of 1960 was career number 275.

#300

Two players joined the impressive 300 home run club in 1960—Eddie Mathews and Mickey Mantle, becoming the 17th and 18th players respectively at that time to do so. The two men actually had a few things in common: both were born in October of 1931 in the same region of the country, Mathews in Texas and Mantle in Oklahoma; Both concluded their careers in 1968; and both also became members of the 500 home run club. Mathews struck his 300th, his first longball of the year, on Easter Sunday, April 17. At the time, he became the second-youngest to reach the figure behind only Jimmie Foxx. Mantle's 300th came on July 4, giving a holiday ring to both blasts.

#350

Though the fine career of Gil Hodges was winding down, he recorded number 350 in '60, occupying the 12th position on

Eddie Mathews. On May 22 of 1960, the Braves' third baseman was presented with the first annual Mel Ott Memorial award for having led the NL in home runs the season before. On August 24 of '60 he became the first NL player to have eight straight 30-home run seasons.

the all-time list at the time. Hodges received the "Lou Gehrig Memorial Award" for spirit and sportsmanship on June 14 of 1960.

#500

Ted Williams reached one of the goals he had looked forward to in Spring Training by joining the extremely exclusive 500 home run club on June 17. The only other members at the time were Ruth, Foxx, and Mel Ott.

With all this in mind, it now seems quite fitting that beginning in the spring of 1960, baseball fans were able to tune into a brand new weekly network television program called "Home Run Derby".

The show was mainly the brainchild of sportscaster Mark Scott, who had broadcast Cincinnati Reds games for one season, and had also worked Pacific Coast League games in the 1950s. Scott collaborated with a Hollywood production company on the project, and in late 1959, the concept for Home Run Derby was born. With Scott as the on-air host, the half-hour show would pit two major league sluggers against each other for a nine-inning "game".

Each contestant would be allowed three outs per inning, with every swing being either a home run or an out. Batting practice pitchers were utilized, and the player with the most home runs at the end of the game was declared the winner, receiving $2,000. The loser came away with $1,000. A bonus system was also in place, whereby a contestant who slugged three consecutive homers would earn an additional $500. With Scott sitting in a booth off to the side commenting on the action, the player who was not batting would sit with him to provide a bit of color and expert commentary.

Filming on the series was set to begin in December of '59, and Wrigley Field in Los Angeles was selected as the "stage". The park had been named after William Wrigley, Jr., who had owned the Pacific Coast League's Los Angeles Angels. In all, 26 episodes were filmed, with the schedule wrapping up in early February of '60. Among the illustrious names who had taken part in the contests were Mantle, Mays, Aaron, Killebrew, Banks, and Frank Robinson, as well as a host of other noteworthy sluggers.

The first installment was a marquee match-up featuring Mantle versus Mays. Willie kicked it off by depositing the first pitch over the left-field wall as former AL umpire Art Passarella signaled "home run". Mantle however, would go on to take the inaugural edition by a score of 9-8 when he knocked out the first pitch in the bottom of the ninth inning. Mantle and Mays both appeared in five episodes of the series, and Mickey had the distinction of also competing on the final show, beating Red Sox outfielder Jackie Jensen in a 13-10 slugfest.

The overall championship in terms of number of appearances and prize money earned went fittingly to homer king Henry Aaron. "Hammerin' Hank" won six of his seven games, bringing

Harmon Killebrew—The powerful slugger would go on to hit 393 home runs in the decade of the Sixties. Said Baltimore catcher Clint Courtney of Killebrew late in the '60 season, "He's got more power than anyone else in the league. He can miss a ball and still hit it out of the park." (National Baseball Library)

home a total of $13,500. Mantle was the runner-up with $10,000 in winnings.

Sadly, Mark Scott passed away from a sudden heart attack in July of 1960, leaving "Home Run Derby" as his most lasting professional achievement. At the time of his death, he, along with actor Jack Webb were attempting to land a Continental League team for Los Angeles.

Filmed appropriately for the era in black and white, the show is beautiful in its simplicity. Commonly seen now on sports cable networks, it allows younger fans to acquaint themselves with several legendary sluggers of an earlier time—to hear them speak and see them swing the bat in their prime. For those who recall viewing the original airings, it remains heartwarmingly nostalgic. The spirit of the show lives on at the turn of the century, with the "Home Run Derby" having become a popular feature of the annual All-Star game festivities in recent years.

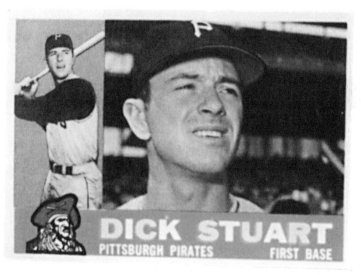

Dick Stuart's 1960 Topps baseball card #402. Stuart took the $6,000 he won on "Home Run Derby" before the '60 season and bought himself a brand new Cadillac. Stuart was the only player in the majors in '60 to have three homers in a game, accomplishing the feat on June 30 versus the Giants. The slugging Stuart was somewhat handicapped by spacious Forbes Field, hitting only eight of his 23 home runs at home that season. (Courtesy, Topps Inc.)

Chapter Eight

Midsummer Classics— Parts I and II

The annual Baseball All-Star Game had been a one-game event from its inception in 1933 until 1959, when it was expanded to a two-game series. The purpose of the additional contest was to raise money for the players' pension fund; however, a lack of interest on the part of both players and fans would cause baseball to revert to the one-game format after 1962.

The first of the two exhibitions of 1960 took place on July 11 at Kansas City for the first time since the Athletics had relocated from Philadelphia in 1955. As it turned out, it would be the only major league All-Star game to ever take place at this park. The two-game set concluded two days later, July 13 at the much more hallowed Yankee Stadium. The contests turned out to be showcases for the impressive all-around skills of Giants center fielder Willie Mays.

Game One was played on a Monday afternoon under the blazing Missouri sun with temperatures reaching 101 degrees. Managers Walt Alston and Al Lopez wisely would not allow any player

Legends Ted Williams and Stan Musial appeared in their last All-Star game together in July of 1960. The two great hitters are posed here in the late 1940s.

to play the entire game due to the extreme heat. American League Chairman of the Board William Harridge handled the duty of tossing out the ceremonial first pitch. He was being recognized for his roles in both the creation of the All-Star game while serving as AL president back in 1933, and also helping to bring major league baseball to Kansas City in 1955.

Mays started things by leading off the game with a triple off Boston right hander Bill Monbouquette. Pirates outfielder Bob Skinner then came up and drove in Mays with a single for a quick 1-0 lead. Two outs later, Ernie Banks homered to make it 3-0 going into the bottom of the first.

Braves catcher Del Crandall hit a solo shot in the second, and Bill Mazeroski singled home Banks in the third to make it 5-0. The Nationals' scoring was over, but the lead would stand. The AL scored an unearned run off the Giants' Mike McCormick in the sixth, and Al Kaline added a two-run homer in the eighth. Mays ended up with a single, double, triple, and one run scored to go along with four putouts in center field in the 5-3 win. Willie's glove had been stolen before the game, and he was forced to use Roy Face's, yet he still managed to thrill the crowd with several patented basket catches.

Switching to New York for Game Two would serve as a bit of a homecoming for Mays. He had not played a game in New York since September of 1957 when the Giants last called the city their home. Mays had actually missed the east coast since the team's departure, and purchased a 15-room stone mansion in New Rochelle, New York in May of '60. Though his jersey bore the strange "San Francisco" across the chest, the performance was like many they remembered from years past.

In his first two at-bats against starter Whitey Ford, Willie singled and homered. He singled later as well for another 3-for-4 day, stole a base, and snagged a team-high five putouts. Eddie Mathews, Stan Musial, and Ken Boyer also homered, and the AL, unable to get anything going, went down to a 6-0 defeat. Musial commented after the game, "This is the most powerful team I've ever seen. Powerful and fast." He also referred to his home run as, " . . . one of the biggest thrills of my career." The main highlight for the junior circuit may have been Ted Williams' pinch-hit single in the seventh in what turned out to be his last All-Star at-bat. The following year, it was Ted who would be throwing out the first pitch at the All-Star game at Fenway Park.

Chapter Nine

R.I.P. Continental League— We Hardly Knew Ye

Throughout the first half of 1960, Organized Baseball was dealing with the very real possibility of the formation of a third major league. History books tend to portray the proposed circuit as a renegade outfit similar to the Federal League's assault on the game back in 1914-'15. The situation however, was clearly quite different.

It appears that the seed was planted for the formation of the "Continental League" by major league owners and executives themselves on May 21, 1959 at a meeting at Pittsburgh Pirates president John Galbreath's farm just outside of Columbus, Ohio. Many of the larger minor league cities had been increasingly applying pressure to the majors to expand in the late 1950s in the wake of the great financial success experienced by teams that had relocated in the previous several years, such as Milwaukee, Baltimore, Los Angeles, and San Francisco. The country's population had been shifting, with much of the growth occurring on the West Coast. Major league owners had previously discussed the possibility of adding two new teams, two more a while later, then splitting the majors into three eight-team leagues. No one seemed in any hurry to pursue this concept.

Baseball Commissioner Ford Frick declared after the May meeting that since there was no current plan to expand, they would "... favorably consider an application for major league status within the present baseball structure by an acceptable group of eight clubs which would qualify under ten specifications."

Among the conditions were a minimum population requirement for each of the proposed cities; stadiums that seated no less than 25,000; and a willingness to adhere to the majors' pension plan, to name a few.

It was at this time that a 38-year-old attorney named William Shea from New York went to work. Shea had previously been appointed by New York Mayor Robert Wagner as chairman of a committee whose goal was to help obtain a new National League franchise for the city in the wake of the departure of the Giants and Dodgers after 1957.

In the two months following Frick's announcement, Shea had more than a dozen cities interested in being part of the group. On July 27, 1959 at the Biltmore Hotel in New York, "The Continental League of Professional Baseball Clubs" was formally announced. Shea had been named chairman of the league's founder's committee, and the five cities already in the fold that were represented at the press conference were New York, Houston, Toronto, Denver, and Minneapolis-St. Paul. Two of the cities' financial backers who were present, Jack Kent Cooke of Toronto and Robert Howsam of Denver, already owned the top-level minor league teams currently competing in their respective cities.

Among the other cites who were vying for a spot in the proposed eight-team circuit were: Buffalo, Montreal, Atlanta, Miami, Indianapolis, Dallas-Ft. Worth, San Diego, Portland, Oregon, Seattle, and San Juan, Puerto Rico.

Shea said at the time that it was the new league's intention to operate within the structure of Organized Baseball, meeting the ten conditions set forth by Frick two months earlier. Each of the cities deposited $50,000 into a league treasury for organizational purposes, and had taken part in drawing up a constitution.

In early August, Continental League officials met with a Senate antitrust committee headed by Senator Estes Kefauver, a Democrat from Tennessee. The committee was looking into possible violations of antitrust laws by organized baseball. Kefauver was seeking to file a bill that would, among other things, limit the number of players controlled by major league teams to 80. Some of the wealthier teams were thought to be controlling upwards of 400 players, and this was seen as a major stumbling block when it came time to stock eight new teams plus their minor league systems.

At the time of the Continental's formation, several prominent baseball men were being considered for the position of president of the league. Branch Rickey, the pioneer of integration was among them. The 77-year-old ex-Dodger general manager was currently serving in an advisory capacity for the Pirates, and was known to support the concept of a third league. Larry MacPhail, former top executive with the Yankees, Dodgers, and Reds was considered a possibility, but quickly took himself out of the running by saying that it was "silly" to try to form a new big league rather than to slowly expand the existing ones. He was quoted as saying, "It seems to me that they would want someone who believes in the formation of a third major league, which I certainly don't."

A couple of weeks later on August 18, 1959, the Continental League formally announced the appointment of Rickey as its president. Reportedly, Shea and his partners had to plead with him to accept the position. Upon selecting Rickey, Shea said, "The position required a man of great dignity, great ability, and a man with a pioneer background." When asked what was his greatest thrill in baseball, Rickey surprisingly said, "I don't think I've come to it yet. This third league may be it." He also stated that he believed the league could be strong enough in three years to compete in a World Series versus the AL and NL. Rickey envisioned that as soon as

1963, the series would be a round-robin affair involving the three leagues.

After unveiling Rickey as their new president, Shea and his group met with officials from Organized Baseball. Present were Commissioner Frick, NL president Warren Giles, AL president Joe Cronin, as well as a small group of owners. The parties explored the means by which the new league would be developed. Frick emphasized that the conditions that were established in May must be adhered to strictly. Representatives of the new circuit were seeking clarification on issues such as acquiring players, territorial rights, pensions, and additional cities to be added.

In mid-October of '59, major league officials discussed a plan whereby the Washington Senators would move to Minnesota; a new expansion team would be placed in Washington; and a new NL team would be placed in New York, thus creating two nine-team leagues and limited inter-league play in the process. On October 21, the AL held a meeting and discussed the possibility of simply adding two expansion franchises, also voting to study a request by a Minneapolis sports committee to be granted an AL team.

Shea responded to these discussions with harsh words: "It's just another move to harass us . . . . " "They were supposed to cooperate with us, but here they are, going in the opposite direction, doing everything to impede us."

In early January 1960, Kefauver expressed disappointment over lack of progress made by the Continentals. Pledging his support, Republican Senator Kenneth Keating of New York said, "I am very much interested in the formation of a new league," and he told Rickey that he would act as informal mediator in negotiations. Both Shea and Rickey indicated that congressional support would help concerning player and territorial rights, as well as dealings with the minor leagues. The chairman of the House Antitrust Subcommittee, Emmanuel Celler, a democrat from Brooklyn also was supportive. A longtime critic of Organized Baseball's 'big business' aspect said if the new circuit encountered difficulties that Congress could assist with, " . . . it would be duty-bound to do so in the interest of the national pastime." Rickey would later declare, "I prefer turbulent progress rather than quiet stagnation."

The New York Times of January 11, 1960 ran a story entitled "Frick predicts rosy future for new league". In it he was quoted as saying "It can't miss. Expansion beyond the present American and National Leagues is inevitable." Frick's sincerity comes into question on this issue as some felt he was merely saying what he had to in order to keep Congress from taking aggressive action.

It was this same month that the Continental League finally rounded out its list of eight clubs, having added Atlanta, Dallas, and lastly, Buffalo. A month later, Rickey attempted to solve his league's player acquisition problem by meeting with officials of the newly reformed Class "D" Western Carolina League about pooling players. In March, Frick announced he would not allow such an arrangement as it would violate existing agreements between the majors and minors. Rickey responded "We have been reduced to obtaining players through the free-agency field."

During mid-April, just as the major league season was getting underway, the proposed New York franchise revealed its plan to build baseball's first retractable-roof domed stadium. They had selected a site in Flushing Meadow, and said that there was a chance it would be ready for Opening Day of the team's inaugural season of 1961.

In early May, Senator Kefauver introduced his bill aimed at solving the new league's problems. The majors held a meeting on May 17 to discuss various aspects of the bill. Frick called it ". . . the most dangerous bill yet introduced in Congress" as far as Organized Baseball was concerned. Shea and his group were, of course, fully behind the measure. Frick and the owners agreed that if the Continentals failed to take positive action soon, including agreeing to suitable indemnity figures for the affected minor leagues, they would proceed with internal expansion.

Branch Rickey was credited with bringing the proposed Continental League closer to reality than anyone would have. Upon its demise, it was written "The CL would have been dead a year ago if not for Rickey's leadership." (National Baseball Library)

Hearings on the bill were held on May 19-20, with several of the key figures appearing. Rickey testified that without legislative action, baseball would never expand beyond its current structure. Frick tried to impress upon the subcommittee how adversely the bill would impact the minor leagues. After studying the testimony for a few days, the committee altered the content of the bill. It eliminated a section that would limit the amount of players controlled by major league teams, and also deleted a section that would have virtually forced the established league to accept the new circuit. It came up for consideration in its new form a month later, on June 28, and the Senate voted 73 to 12 to send it back to the judiciary committee. The bill then became bogged down and never did come up again for consideration.

By midsummer, the Continentals were considering delaying the start of their first season until 1962. Meanwhile, the AL secretly discussed expansion at meetings in Kansas City and New York on July 10-11 in conjunction with the season's two All-Star games. The owners agreed to expand as soon as NL owners decided on expansion for their league. A week later, on July 18, the NL voted unanimously to expand to ten teams if the new league didn't begin to achieve its goals. They then issued a warning to the Continentals that if they didn't make progress very soon, including paying the indemnity fees, the NL would take a few of their proposed cities as their own future expansion sites.

The Continentals met in New York on July 20-21 to discuss the indemnification fees that they would need to pay to the International League, American Association, and Southern Association. The amount offered was immediately rejected by all three minor leagues, and Shea's group had just about reached the end of the line. The league's official demise came at a meeting at Chicago's Conrad Hilton Hotel on August 2, 1960. Rickey and his group accepted the proposition at this time that four of their cities would be included in the upcoming expansion, though Toronto would ultimately be replaced by Los Angeles. So the Continental League, of which Rickey had declared eight months earlier "...as sure as tomorrow morning" was off the drawing board.

It is somewhat ironic that the minor league system that Rickey had helped to create nearly four decades earlier would turn out to be one of his major stumbling blocks in the creation of the new league. Shea, on the other hand, was pleased because he had succeeded in his mission of bringing another major league team to New York. The city would show its gratitude by naming the Mets' new stadium after him in 1964.

It is interesting to speculate how the course of baseball history may have been drastically altered had the Continentals succeeded in getting off the ground. Even in failing, it indirectly led to the historic expansion the game experienced in 1961 and '62.

Chapter Ten

---

27 Innings, No Hits— 3 No-No's

When a major league pitcher is set for his day's work—his warmup tosses have been completed, the umpire hollers "Play ball!," and the lead off hitter steps in, likely one of the last things on his mind is the probability of holding every batter he faces hitless over the next nine innings. It is hardly worth dwelling on the remote possibility that his repertoire of pitches may be so dominating that not one major league hitter he is challenged by on this day will reach base via home run, solid line drive, or fluky scratch single. Yet three pitchers defied the odds and joined this exclusive club during the season of 1960.

When Chicago Cubs vice-president John Holland decided to acquire 24-year-old pitcher Don Cardwell in a trade with the Phillies on May 13, he had no way of knowing how quickly dividends would be paid. Two days later, Cardwell made his Cubs debut and made Holland look like a genius.

It was the second game of a Sunday afternoon doubleheader versus rival St. Louis with 33,543 in attendance at Wrigley Field. After retiring the leadoff batter, Cardwell went three and two on Alex Grammas before losing him with a walk. From then on it was clear sailing with no more batters reaching base—seven going down on strikes. Ernie Banks helped with a home run in the 4-0 game, and first baseman Ed Bouchee, who came over from the Phils in the trade along with Cardwell made 11 putouts. The game would be the highlight of Cardwell's 14-year career.

On August 18 it was Braves veteran right hander Lew Burdette's turn in the spotlight; however, he was no stranger to big accomplishments. The 11-year vet had twice won 20 games; had led the NL in ERA; and had gone 3-0 in the 1957 World Series, including a 5-0 shutout in the clinching seventh game, earning the series MVP award.

On this Tuesday night at County Stadium in Milwaukee, Burdette would be just one hit-batsman away from a perfect game over the Phillies. It was center fielder Tony Gonzalez who got in the way of a Burdette fastball in the fifth inning to become the only Philadelphia baserunner. In all, big Lew needed only 91 pitches to complete his gem. Aside from mastery on the mound, he also was effective with his bat, going two for three. After leading off the eighth with a double, Burdette was driven home by outfielder Bill Bruton's double to score the game's only run. The day after the no-hitter, Burdette received a telegram from presidential candidate John Kennedy that read, "Congratulations on your fine pitching perfor-mance last night. If I can learn your technique, I might possibly throw a no-hitter in November."

Though it was the only no-hitter Lew would ever throw, it was not the only near-perfect contest he was ever involved in. Fif-teen months earlier, he had actually gotten the 1-0 complete game shutout victory in Pirate Harvey Haddix's 12-inning perfect game that was lost in the 13th inning.

Twenty-nine days after Burdette's gem with the same Phillies at the same County Stadium, Warren Spahn displayed his own hit-less dominance. Unfortunately, rain that afternoon and the threat of more that evening kept the crowd to only 6,117, the second-smallest since the Braves moved to Milwaukee. Spahn however, really put on a show for the faithful, striking out a career-high 15, and capturing his 20th win of the season in grand style. He said afterward, "I couldn't let old Lew get away with a no-hitter. I had to go out and pitch one myself." The Phillies had now been no-hit for the tenth time of the century—more than any other team. With 287 career wins at this time, Spahn was the active leader, a distinction he would not relinquish until his retirement in 1965.

All-time winningest left-hander Warren Spahn. Joe Garagiola said of Spahn in the summer of '60, "If I were a kid bent on being a pitcher . . . I'd study Warren Spahn—everything he does, and most of all, his moves." Around that same time, Stan Musial called him the best pitcher he'd ever seen. On July 15 he racked up his 2,000th strikeout. On August 30 he hurled his 50th career shutout. Also a great hitting pitcher, Spahn broke the NL record for home runs by a pitcher with his 25th on August 26. (National Baseball Library)

Chapter Eleven

Jackie's Legacy Grows

On April 9 and 10 of 1960, the Boston Red Sox and Cleveland Indians played two exhibition games at City Park Stadium in New Orleans, Louisiana. What is worth noting about these seemingly insignificant games is that for the first time in this city in the deep South, black fans were allowed to sit amongst whites in the stands.

The Sporting News of April 20 included an article about the event, reporting, "There were no incidents of any kind among the spectators. White fans applauded the slugging of Walter Bond, the Indians' big colored outfielder as vigorously as Negro spectators cheered the hitting of Tito Francona, also of Cleveland."

With regard to race relations within the realm of major league baseball, the times were most definitely changing.

In early 1960, *Sport Magazine* had assembled several noteworthy black athletes at a private dining room at the Biltmore Hotel in New York and engaged them in a roundtable discussion on the progress of the black athlete in America. Both Jackie Robinson and Larry Doby, pioneering figures in the field, were on hand representing a baseball perspective. The meeting resulted in an article in the magazine's March, 1960 issue entitled "The Negro in American Sport."

Both Doby and Robinson agreed that black athletes had come a long, long way in terms of their acceptance by the sports-viewing public. Doby felt that winning now took precedent over the color of the performers. "Everybody loves a winner," he said. "If you have nine Negroes on a ball club, and they're winning, they'll love them." Robinson observed that sports could be a common denominator between athletes, saying, "I know that white players seek out Negro players in Spring Training and try to cultivate friendships with them because they have things in common."

The piece also pointed out that back in 1947 the Cardinals had a rule that restricted black fans to the right field stands. When Robinson's Dodgers were in town, the right field stands would be overflowing, while there were many empty seats in nearly every other section of the park. Management eventually realized the absurdity and lifted the ban.

Commenting on the *Sport Magazine* piece, *The Sporting News*, recognizing the game's progress, editorialized, "But baseball, in less than 15 years since Jackie Robinson first broke down the barriers, has made tremendous strides which might well be the envy of persons in other professions."

In Spring Training of '60, St. Louis Cardinals pinch-hitter extraordinaire George Crowe commented on the progress of blacks in the majors. "Our players have made steady and substantial progress, and we've had our share of batting champions and Most Valuable Player winners. Scouts are on the lookout for good colored players just as they are for good white players, and when they do come up, the colored boy gets the same opportunity."

Ernest Mehl, baseball writer for the *Kansas City Star* wrote in late August, "There is no longer any feeling in the matter, and we don't know of any organization, including the Athletics, that would not jump at the chance to get a Negro player who had the talent to be used regularly."

Boston center fielder Willie Tasby, playing in a city and for a team with less than stellar track records in these matters said in all sincerity in late July, "Everybody in Boston has been wonderful to me." Dale Long, a white player who played with San Francisco until a late-season trade to the Yankees referred to the racial harmony he experienced on the Giants that year. "The whites and Negroes and Latin Americans were always kidding around with one another. Nobody hated anybody. I thought we all mixed pretty good."

When Alvin Dark was hired as the manager of the Giants on October 31, 1960, he was asked at the press conference if the team had too many "colored players". He responded, "Because I'm from the South, people might think I'm prejudiced against them. To get the true answers, why not ask those I've played with on the Giants—Willie Mays, Monte Irvin, Hank Thompson, Ray Noble. I got along fine with them." Dark also added that he had been listening to the Kennedy-Nixon debates recently, and said, "I heard them say it's the man who counts, not his color. I agree that skill is the standard. You can't separate ballplayers."

The separation of ballplayers in an earlier time brought about the Negro Leagues, and remarkably, the Negro American League still existed during the summer of 1960. The circuit was literally on its last legs, having dwindled down to just four teams. They included the Kansas City Monarchs, Birmingham Black Barons, Detroit-New Orleans Stars, and Raleigh Tigers. With virtually no legitimate major league prospect being denied the opportunity at a job in organized pro ball at that juncture, the four remaining teams had to settle for lower-quality players. With interest all but gone, the league's 28th annual East-West All-Star Game at Comiskey Park on August 21 of that year would be its last. Decades before, this summer exhibition was primarily the best opportunity for fans to witness the country's best black baseball talent assembled on one field. By the summer of 1960, one needed only to tune in his tele-

Minnie Minoso of the Chicago White Sox, who had competed in the Negro Leagues back in the mid-1940s. Minnie didn't debut in the majors until he was nearly 27 years old, and went on to be regarded as the best all-around left-fielder in the American League in the decade of the 1950s. (National Baseball Library)

vision from the comfort of his living room to see the major league All-Star Game featuring the likes of Mays, Aaron, Clemente, Cepeda, Minoso, and others. After the '60 season, the Kansas City Monarchs, one of the most noteworthy of the Negro League's teams, went out of business. With black ballplayers now fully ingrained into mainstream baseball, it is fitting that for all intents and purposes, this marked the end of Negro league baseball as it was known.

After Jackie Robinson had changed the complexion of major league baseball in April of 1947, four other black players followed that season. Very slowly but steadily, teams throughout the majors were integrating their rosters, and by the end of 1957, only Detroit and the Red Sox remained the last vestiges of lily-white baseball.

In 1958, Detroit finally threw a dash of color into the team by bringing in third baseman Ozzie Virgil, which rendered the Red Sox the lone holdout. Finally, a full 14 years after Jackie Robinson had been given a sham of a tryout at Fenway Park along with Sam Jethroe and Marvin Davis, the Red Sox ushered in a new era with Elijah "Pumpsie" Green at second base. Two more black players, Earl Wilson and Willie Tasby would join Green on the Boston roster in 1960. By '60, the novelty of an integrated major league had worn off to the degree that nearly 90 players appeared that season who wouldn't have even been considered for the major leagues by virtue of the color of their skin as recently as 14 years prior.

With the challenge of introducing black players onto the major league landscape now met, the next frontier was thought to be the position of field manager. *The Sporting News* took a bold stand and editorialized on the subject in their August 24 issue in 1960. "Someday there will be in the not too far away a Negro manager in the majors, and coaches too. Men like Crowe, Banks, [Earl] Battey, [Elston] Howard seem to have the leadership qualities. If they have the talent and desire, they should not be denied."

Barriers had already been broken within the area of baseball scouting. Former Kansas City Monarchs star first baseman and manager John "Buck" O'Neil, who had become the majors' first black scout was still working for the Chicago Cubs. In June of '60, Piper Davis, former Negro league teammate of Willie Mays became the first black scout in Tiger history.

Major league teams were beginning to reject the racist practices that were still in effect in the South. The Nashville minor league team of the Southern Association lost its working agreement with the Cincinnati Reds due to the fact that it didn't allow black players on the team. Other teams in the league had previously been affected for this reason as well.

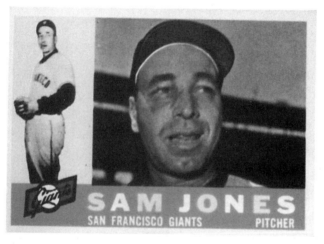

Sam Jones' 1960 Topps card #410. The lanky right-hander had led the NL in wins once, ERA once, and strikeouts three times. In 1955 he became the first black pitcher to throw a no-hitter in the major leagues and would clearly have been the NL Cy Young award winner in '59 had the award been given out in both leagues. In 1960 he threw one one-hitter, two two-hitters, three three-hitters, one four-hitter, and one five-hitter. NL MVP Dick Groat, describing Jones' assortment of curveballs in July of '60 said, "He's got a dozen curves. He has fast curves, slow curves, about six different speeds, and they all break quick." (Courtesy Topps Inc.)

Vic Power's 1960 Topps card #75. A magician with a first baseman's mitt, Joe Gordon called him the greatest of all time at the position defensively. Power would win the Gold Glove in the AL in the first seven years of the award's existence ('58-'64). (Courtesy Topps Inc.)

Vada Pinson—Turning 22 during the 1960 season, he was already one of the best center fielders in either league. With his tremendous ability in all phases of the game, former Braves manager Fred Haney predicted that he could turn out even better than Mays, Aaron, Mantle, or Kaline. Gabe Paul said, "All I know is, I've never seen a more exciting picture in baseball than Pinson turning on the speed and running a single into a double." The Saturday Evening Post *of July 16, 1960 featured an article on Pinson entitled, "Is he the Nearest-Perfect Player?" (National Baseball Library)*

Other than the top-echelon black stars such as Mays, Aaron, Banks, etc., several others were distinguishing themselves on the field in several outstanding ways at the dawn of the decade. Crowe of the Cardinals had set a major league record in June of '60 for pinch-hit home runs with 11, and had extended it by year's end to 14. Maury Wills' 50 stolen bases was the highest total in the National League since Max Carey swiped that many back in 1923. And Orlando Cepeda so impressed old-time Southerner Ty Cobb that he said in September, "If he is not the equal of Willie Mays, he soon will be."

Youngsters Vada Pinson, Bob Gibson, Billy Williams, Curt Flood, and so many more ensured that brilliant living color was now a permanent part of the game.

Chapter Twelve

Game Bids Goodbye to Two Old-Time Greats

On the morning of August 14 of 1960, the Pittsburgh Pirates were on their way to their surprising NL championship, sporting a four-game lead over second-place St. Louis. That Sunday afternoon, the Bucs captured both ends of a doubleheader over the Cardinals to increase the margin to six games. That evening as the team was basking in the joy of the dual victory, Fred Clarke, one of the most famous old Pirates from the team's most glorious period passed away at 87 years of age.

Clarke had made his major league debut way back in 1894 as an outfielder with the Louisville Colonels of the National League. In 1900 the Colonels and Pittsburgh merged, retaining the Pirate name, with Clarke named as the team's player-manager. Joining him from Louisville were future Hall of Famers Honus Wagner and pitcher Rube Waddell.

Under Clarke, a highly productive hitter himself, the Pirates finished second in 1900, but won three consecutive pennants from '01 through '03. It was in 1903 that Pittsburgh participated in the first modern-day world series, losing to Cy Young's Boston Americans in eight games. They again recorded second-place finishes in 1905, '07, and '08, but Clarke and company finally brought home a world championship banner in 1909 by defeating Ty Cobb's Detroit Tigers.

Clarke retired as both an active player and manager after the 1915 season, having compiled extremely impressive accomplishments in each role. As one of the premier left fielders of his time, he slugged a whopping 220 triples, still seventh best of all-time, and finished with a .312 career batting average. In his 16 seasons as manager, his .595 career winning percentage tops all Pirate skippers. Beyond Clarke's statistical impact on the game, he is also credited with devising the first tarpaulin to cover the infield during the latter portion of his career.

The ultimate honor of being inducted into the Baseball Hall of Fame was deservedly bestowed upon Clarke in 1945. At the time of his passing in 1960, he was the oldest living ex-player to have received the honor. Clarke rooted for the Pirates until his dying day, and said shortly before his death, "This is the year we are going to do it. I can feel it."

Less than three months after Clarke's death, Bobby Wallace, a contemporary from the NL in the 1890s, also died. One of the outstanding defensive shortstops of his day, Wallace had debuted with the Cardinals the same year Clarke broke in, 1894, and did not conclude his playing career until 1918. His 25-season career also included a 15-season stay with the St. Louis Browns of the American League, and a brief stint as an AL umpire. Wallace joined Clarke in the Hall of Fame in 1953.

While the baseball world lost these two hallowed figures in 1960, it gained a few future stars with the births that year of Tony Gwynn, Cal Ripken, Jr., Joe Carter, and John Franco.

Chapter Thirteen

Managerial Maneuvering

Judging from the progression of events during 1960, major league managers could well have been regarded as an endangered species. Of the 16 teams that competed that season, eight teams, a full 50 percent, made at least one managerial change during the calendar year.

Beyond the fact that so many changes were made, it was the sometimes bizarre nature in which they were made that is worth examining.

The National League's Opening Day came on April 12, and the first change, unusual because of the timing, was set to occur. Phillies manager Eddie Sawyer saw his team drop its first game 9-4 to the Cincinnati Reds, and realizing he had no desire to be part of what was certain to be a miserably long season, he resigned the next day. Phils coach Andy Cohen took over for one game until Gene Mauch was hired to begin his long, distinguished managerial career.

Four weeks later on May 4, the Cubs fired Charlie Grimm, who had just begun his third stint as the team's field boss. The 61-year-old Grimm had played with the Cubs for the last 12 years of his 21-year playing career, and served as their manager from 1932 to '38, and from '44 through '49. Grimm's advancing age brought on physical difficulties, and many felt he didn't handle the pitching staff well. Cubs vice-president John Holland knew a change was inevitable on April 17, when in the eighth inning of a tight game, Grimm had pitcher Don Elston bat with two out and a runner on third. Chicago writer Milton Gross subsequently wrote that the game had passed Grimm by.

The unusual aspect of his dismissal was that he was replaced by Cubs radio broadcaster Lou Boudreau, who had been behind the microphone for three seasons. Grimm in turn took Boudreau's place in the booth, in what amounted to the trade of a manager for a color commentator.

A questionable tactical move on the part of Red Sox manager Billy Jurges on June 7 may well have been the last straw that led to his removal as well. In a game that day versus Cleveland, he made a desperate move by putting outfielder Bobby Thomson at first base, when he had never played the position. Jurges had two other players—Pete Runnels and Marty Keough—available who had played it, but chose Thomson, who used a regular fielder's glove and made two errors. With the team playing very poorly, the embattled Jurges took a leave of absence the next day, as coach Del Baker took over on an interim basis. Though Jurges had been given the dreaded vote of confidence from Boston management twice in recent weeks, he was officially terminated as Mike Higgins was hired on June 12.

Just six days after Higgins' hiring, the San Francisco Giants made news by firing manager Bill Rigney. They replaced him for the duration of the season with 66-year-old lifelong baseball man Tom Sheehan, who had never managed in the majors. The Giants were in second place, only four games behind league-leading Pittsburgh at the time of the change, and some called it a panic move on the part of Giants owner Horace Stoneham. Rigney had improved the team's winning percentage each year since taking over in 1956.

Though Giants players liked Sheehan, they seemed to lack confidence and respect for him. By season's end, it turned out to be a giant mistake, as the team finished 16 games back.

August 3 brought what was likely the most bizarre managerial change of the entire year, perhaps even the century. It was this day that the Cleveland Indians and Detroit Tigers announced that they would be swapping managers in an even-up trade. Joe Gordon would take over the Tigers, while Detroit manager Jimmie Dykes was to be the new Indians skipper. *The Sporting News* called the move, "the latest in a season of unusual events." Pat Harmon of the *Cincinnati Post* and *Times-Star* wrote, "Baseball managers have something new to worry about now. They might be traded. Formerly, all they had to worry about was (a) getting fired; (b) getting fined; or (c) getting punched in the nose by one of their own players."

It all began in early July when Tigers president Bill DeWitt and Cleveland G.M. Frank Lane were discussing trades and getting nowhere. DeWitt finally said to Lane facetiously, "Let's trade managers," to which Lane replied, "Your team is going nowhere and so is ours. Maybe it wouldn't be a bad idea." The historic transaction was made official weeks later and positively stunned the baseball world. One unnamed observer stated, "You can almost depend on Lane to be involved in anything that's bizarre and freakish. Bill Veeck must be envious. Why didn't he think of this?" After the trade, Dykes blasted DeWitt for his interference, his visits to the clubhouse, and telegrams with suggestions. Dykes had first managed in the majors with the White Sox back in 1934, and was now setting a record by piloting his fifth big-league team.

As a postscript to the deal, on October 3, the day after the season ended, Joe Gordon announced he would be stepping down as Tigers manager to take over the Kansas City Athletics. Gordon cited DeWitt's meddling as a factor, which had a familiar ring to it, and also said he realized that the Tigers weren't as good as he thought. As bad as Detroit may have been, Kansas City was considerably worse, and Gordon was replaced by Hank Bauer after 59 games in the 1961 season.

After Gordon's resignation, the Tigers announced the hiring of Bob Scheffing as manager on November 21. Scheffing had managed the Cubs from 1957 through '59, and would become Detroit's eighth manager since 1954.

The day after Gordon quit the Tigers, the carnage continued when the Cubs announced that Lou Boudreau would not return as manager, but would resume his work in the radio booth. Two weeks later, just five days after the conclusion of the World Series, one of the most major managerial stories broke. The Yankees decided to put an end to the historic reign of Casey Stengel as the Pinstripes skipper after 12 memorable seasons. Stengel turned 70 in mid-season and had missed several games due to a hospital stay. Age and health were Yankee management's big concern. Yankee coach and former back-up catcher Ralph Houk, who was thought to be groomed as Stengel's successor for some time was named for the pressure-filled position days later. He then began a very noteworthy 20-year managerial career of his own. As for Stengel, many organizations were thought to be pursuing his services in the coming weeks.

A week and a half later on Halloween Day, the San Francisco Giants attempted to correct their situation by hiring Alvin Dark to lead the team on the field. Dark had played third base and the outfield with the Milwaukee Braves in '60, and at this time the Giants traded outfielder Andre Rodgers even up for him for the purpose of naming him their new manager. This marked the end of Dark's 14-year playing career and the beginning of his equally impressive 13-year managerial career.

Aside from the eight teams that had made managerial changes from April to October, two other teams made hirings that were not brought on by firings. In each case, however, there was no manager to fire. The new expansion team in Washington, D.C. selected old-time Senator Mickey Vernon to pilot their new edition, while the new Los Angeles franchise plucked Bill Rigney from the unemployment line to get their team off the ground.

Finally, a year that saw so many unusual twists and turns regarding the field bosses throughout the majors ended with possibly the most unusual move of all. Cubs owner Phil Wrigley, who had already contributed to the odd occurrences made an unprecedented decision during the last week of December. Wrigley's revolutionary concept called for a staff of eight coaches who would rotate managerial duties throughout the 1961 season. The details of who and how were to be determined in the coming weeks, but one need only look at the Cubs' 64-90 record in '61 to evaluate the effectiveness of the plan.

Not only was the job of major league manager an extremely tenuous one in 1960, it was hard to predict the direction from which his replacement might be coming.

Chapter Fourteen

"Beat 'em Bucs"!
—A Banner for Steel City

It wasn't until 1958 that the Pirates had begun to emerge from the doldrums in which they had wallowed for the majority of the 1950s. In the eight-season span from 1950 through '57 the team had finished in last place six times; next-to-last the other two seasons, winning 454 of the 1,231 games they had played. Danny Murtaugh had taken over as manager of the team in August of 1957, and under the first full season of his leadership in '58, they shocked the league with 84 wins and a second-place finish. They slipped back a bit in 1959 with a 78-76 record, good for only fourth place. Having been dubiously regarded a few years earlier as the "St. Louis Browns of the National League," Pittsburgh was ready to put the worst decade in their 88-year history behind them.

In the early spring of 1960 when the media began making predictions for the upcoming season, there was generally not a lot of optimism regarding the Pirates' pennant chances. The general feeling was that a lack of power and a shortage of top pitching would keep them out of the race. Esteemed *Sporting News* editor J. G. Taylor Spink went on record as predicting a fifth-place finish. One of the lone Pirate supporters was *New York Daily News* maverick Dick Young, who had the foresight to pick them to finish first.

Manager Murtaugh, a 42-year-old native and resident of Chester, Pennsylvania had once worn the Pirates uniform himself back in his playing days. In a nine-year career that ended in 1951, the former second baseman had spent his final four seasons in the Pittsburgh infield. The Irishman was a tobacco-chewing, even-tempered sort, hailed for his patience and ability to handle all types of men and get the most out of them. He was entering the 1960 season with a team on which the average age of the starting eight position players was 28. Though relatively youthful collectively, there was no shortage of big-league experience. Even the youngest, second-base defensive whiz Bill Mazeroski at only 23 was entering his fifth major league season.

The pitching staff was led by ordained Mormon minister Vern Law, of whom Pittsburgh writer Les Biederman would call in June of 1960, "the least-publicized yet probably the best all-around pitcher in the game today." Bob Friend had pitched for the Pirates since he was a 20-year-old rookie back in 1951. He compiled a terrific 22-14 record in 1958, but was now trying to rebound from a disastrous 8-19 record in '59. Bullpen ace Roy Face had authored the staggering distinction of 18 wins in relief versus only one defeat in '59. Largely on the strength of that outstanding campaign, the 5'8", 155 lb. Face was reportedly the highest-paid Pirate in '60 at $35,000. Other Pirates poised to make a mark this season were slugging first baseman Dick Stuart, though his nickname "Dr. Strangeglove" speaks volumes about his defensive shortcomings; left fielder Bob Skinner, beginning to be recognized as one of the better left-handed hitters in the league; shortstop Dick Groat, on the verge of his career year; and Roberto Clemente, who would come through with statistical highs to that point in several categories.

On Opening Day 1960, Face took the loss against the Braves, a sharp contrast to the previous season when it wasn't until September 11 that he was tagged with his one and only defeat. Despite the setback in the opener, Pittsburgh went on to win 12 of their first

15, a stretch that included a nine-game winning streak. In the most noteworthy game of that span on April 17, back-up catcher Hal Smith's pinch-hit three-run homer contributed to a six-run ninth inning in a 6-5 win over the Reds. They continued to play inspired baseball, and remained at or near the top of the NL through May. Clemente was leading the team on the field, and was voted the league's Player of the Month for May. At a pre-game ceremony in June, legendary Pirates third baseman "Pie" Traynor presented Clemente with a desk set from Warren Giles for earning the honor. In broken English, Robert predicted a Pirate pennant for the Forbes Field crowd. It was at this time that Pittsburgh general manager Joe L. Brown stated that amongst all right fielders in the NL including Aaron, Clemente was the best.

The Bucs were beginning to establish a reputation for incredible late-inning heroics leading to come-from-behind victories. One noteworthy example was June 18 in Los Angeles, with Dodgers Danny McDevitt within one strike of a 3-0 three-hitter with no one on base. A couple of batters later, Hal Smith homered, sending the game into extra innings. Smith came back in the tenth and singled in a run for the 4-3 win. After the game, L.A., third base coach Bobby Bragan, who had managed Pittsburgh in 1956 and '57 called them a "team of destiny." Some believed at the time that if the Pirates did go on to capture the pennant, this particular victory could well have been the turning point. It gave them the largest lead any NL team had in the past two years.

On July 6 at Crosley Field in Cincinnati, Bob Skinner hit an inside-the-park grand slam in the eighth inning for a 5-2 win. Two-and-a-half weeks later on July 24 with their loss to the Giants in San Francisco, the Pirates dropped out of first place for the first time since May 30. Bob Friend came right back the next day to defeat St. Louis, leapfrogging Pittsburgh back over Milwaukee for the top spot. In late August, Pirates' beat writer Harry Keck marveled, "Almost nightly, Manager Danny Murtaugh's never-say-die cliffhangers pull rabbits out of hats and manipulate mirrors to snatch games out of the fire."

The Pirates' pennant aspirations would be put to the test by an errant Lew Burdette pitch on September 6. Shortstop and team captain Dick Groat, who hadn't missed an inning all season had his left wrist broken by the big Milwaukee right-hander. It was feared that he might not only miss the rest of the season, but also the World Series should they hang on to first place. The loss was potentially devastating to Pittsburgh, as Groat was outstanding batting second in the order, and was recognized as the best hit-and-run man in the NL. Edgar Munzel of the *Chicago Sun-Times* wrote a week before Groat's wrist was broken that he was the field general of the Pirates just as Alvin Dark was to the '48 Braves or Nellie Fox was of the '59 White Sox. Dick Young wrote at that time that he should receive strong support for MVP. Vern Law also testified to Groat's extraordinary hit-and-run ability, and added, " . . . he's a better shortstop now than he's ever been. We could never be this far out in front without Groat." One of his more noteworthy performances of the season came on May 13 at Milwaukee as he went six for six in an 8-2 win. Also on June 12 versus St. Louis, he had four hits in the first four innings. The shortstop graced the cover of the August 8 issue of *Sports Illustrated* under the title "Fiery Leader of the Pirates."

With Groat out, Murtaugh had to shift his batting order around. Switch-hitting Dick Schofield took over at shortstop and produced well, with ten hits in his first 23 at-bats over seven games. Third baseman Don Hoak would be assuming the role of team captain in Groat's absence.

Pennant fever had positively overtaken the city of Pittsburgh by early September. Despite railroad strikes and steel industry strikes, the Pirates were the biggest story in town. A song called "Beat 'em Bucs" was a popular tune in the city, with the slogan plastered all over store windows, delivery trucks, and city buses. After not having won a pennant since 1927, Pittsburgh fans could not contain their excitement.

Staff ace Vern Law achieved a personal milestone on September 18 with his 20th victory of the year, though it took him four attempts to do so. It would turn out to be the only season he reached the plateau in his 16-year career. Law was, in a sense, the Pirates' "stopper". During the 1960 season, the team had only two four-game losing streaks, and each time, Law was the pitcher to halt the streak.

The cast was removed from Groat's left wrist on September 19, and his doctor gave him permission to begin swinging a bat. The team was hopeful that he would be ready for postseason play. Reminding reporters of his value to the team, Murtaugh stated that Groat's .325 batting average didn't begin to tell the story. Said the manager, "He's a leader in his quiet, inspirational way and has been worth his weight in gold to us this season."

Finally, on September 25, the day that Pirates fans had waited for arrived. They were in Milwaukee playing the Braves in an afternoon game when word came from Chicago at 2:45 P.M. It was the seventh inning with Pittsburgh holding a 1-0 lead, and Clemente in the batter's box. The announcement came that the Cubs had just beaten the Cardinals, which clinched the pennant for Pittsburgh. That the Pirates lost the game to the Braves on Eddie Mathews' two-run home run in the tenth inning for their third consecutive loss was now irrelevant. A crowd of 200,000 cheering Pittsburgh fans greeted the new NL champs as they returned home that evening. The fans supported their Bucs very well all year, and would set a team record for attendance at 1,705,828. They also learned that day who the Pirates' World Series opponents would be as the Yankees' victory in Boston assured a rematch of the 1927 Fall Classic.

Groat revealed at this time that he first began believing in the Bucs' pennant chances in mid-June when they swept three from the Giants at Candlestick, then took two of three in L.A. He said, "We came home with a four-game lead, and after looking over the

The 1960 Pittsburgh Pirates, the team that brought the World Series to Forbes Field for the fourth and final time. Entertainer Bing Crosby owned approximately $250,000 worth of stock in the team. Four players on this team had sons who went on to play major league baseball themselves— Vern Law, Bob Skinner, Dick Schofield, and Fred Green. (National Baseball Library)

league, I decided we were as good, if not better, than any other team." Groat came back from his wrist injury on September 27 versus the Reds, and played in the final few games of the season. The Pirates closed out the campaign with a drastically overachieving 95-57 record, seven games ahead of second-place Milwaukee. Having regained first place on July 25 after dropping out for one day, Pittsburgh held on the rest of the way. In all, they had spent 146 days in the top spot.

A review of team statistics shows that the Pirates scored more total runs than any other NL team, while tying the Giants for allowing the fewest. Their league-best team batting average of .276 eclipsed the second-best team by 11 points, and percentage-wise,

Pittsburgh also topped the league defensively. One element that wasn't part of the Pirates game was speed, as their 34 stolen bases as a team ranked last in the league. The pitching staff however, did itself a favor by walking the fewest batters of any team in the majors by a considerable margin.

Individually there were several noteworthy achievements. Groat captured the batting title with a .325 average, finishing six points above runner-up Mays. It marked the first time in 25 years that a shortstop had won the NL batting crown since Arky Vaughan—also of the Pirates—had accomplished the feat. Going into the 2000 season, no other NL shortstop has achieved the distinction.

Roberto Clemente's outstanding season included placing third in the batting race at .314, and his powerful throwing arm enabled him to lead all major league outfielders in assists with 19. Vern Law tied for the major league lead in complete games with 18, and compiled an impressive three-to-one strikeout-to-walk ratio. Murtaugh pulled it all together and was rewarded after the season as the NL Manager of the Year by a wide margin over the Cardinals' Solly Hemus. Pirate general manager Joe L. Brown was given credit for having traded for Don Hoak, Bill Virdon, Smoky Burgess, Rocky Nelson, and starting pitchers Harvey Haddix and Vinegar Bend Mizell. Branch Rickey was acknowledged as well for having brought in Groat, Skinner, Stuart, Clemente, Mazeroski, and Face during his tenure as G.M. in the first half of the 1950s.

The Pirates had waited 33 years to avenge their loss in their last World Series appearance, a sweep at the hands of the mighty '27 Yankees. On October 5, the process would begin at Forbes Field, with most interesting and unusual results.

Chapter Fifteen

25th Flag Flies at Ruth's House

The magical ride that Casey Stengel had been on since assuming managerial control of the Yankees in 1949 had hit rough going a decade later. After having piloted nine pennant winners in ten seasons, Stengel found his team at the close of 1959 in third place, just four games over .500, and a distant 15 games behind the AL champion White Sox.

As a result, the 69-year-old skipper was very cautious in Spring Training of 1960 not to predict a pennant as he did the previous Spring. Mickey Mantle was coming off his worst season yet in terms of runs batted in with only 75, and he was also being plagued by an inflamed right knee this spring and was unable to train hard. He also had to suffer the indignity of a $4,000 pay cut from $70,000 to $66,000. Stengel also wasn't fully confident in his mind that the Yankees had come out even in the Roger Maris trade, but indicated that he would wait until after the season to evaluate it fully.

Longtime Yankee outfielder Hank Bauer, among those shipped to Kansas City for Maris showed his old team he could still produce by going five for six with five RBI in his first Spring Training game against them on March 21 at St. Petersburg. Bauer would be managing the Athletics by the following season. Regarding Maris, Stengel intended to switch him to left field, moving Hector Lopez over to right. Ever the team player, Maris responded, "If Stengel feels that the welfare of the club demands my shifting to left, then left it will be." The switch lasted throughout most of Spring Training, but was reversed just before the season began. Stengel was also experimenting with Yogi Berra at third base, but ultimately settled on 23-year-old Clete Boyer as the starter. There was also considerable youth in the middle of the infield with 23-year-old Tony Kubek at shortstop and Bobby Richardson, 25 at second. Veteran of many championships, Moose Skowron was holding down first base and hoping for his first injury-free season in several years.

The Yankees had a very lackluster spring, and few analysts viewed them as serious contenders. They dropped their final Florida contest 7-4 to Cleveland for an 11-21 spring record, and Joe Trimble of the *New York Daily News* wrote, "The Yankees waved bye-bye to Florida today in just about the same fashion they spent the spring. That is, by getting the daylights beat out of them." Another observer remarked, "This was the worst Yankee team that ever came out of Florida. They looked worse than the club that stumbled home third in 1959."

With a small cloud of skepticism hanging over their pennant aspirations, the Yankees were at Fenway Park on April 19 to officially begin the quest. Wearing the number nine on his road gray Yankee flannels, young Maris made quite an impression in the opener. Batting in the lead off position he went four-for-five with two home runs, a double, a single, and four RBI in New York's 8-4 win. Three days later on April 22, the Yankees held their home opener at the Stadium versus the Orioles. Whitey Ford, pitching the first seven innings, and Ralph Terry the final two, combined on a 5-0 shutout. Mantle slugged a home run, and after walking, scored the 1,000th run of his career. In the third game of the Orioles series on April 24, the Yankees tied a record by scoring eight runs in the first inning before the first out was recorded. Though Baltimore came back with grand slams in both the eighth and ninth innings, New York held on to win the eventful game 15-9. Six days later in their final game of April, they pummeled the Orioles 16-0.

New York had won six of their first ten games and were sitting on top of the league on May 1. Mediocrity crept in during the month of May, however, as the team compiled a record of 13-13. By the morning of June 1, they had slipped to fourth.

It was also around this date that Detroit had reportedly offered Rocky Colavito in exchange for Mickey Mantle, but were quickly rebuffed. Stengel had been stricken with a viral infection that required hospitalization on May 29, and wasn't able to return to the team until June 7. In his absence, Ralph Houk assumed the managerial duties. Many on the team believed that Houk would be taking over when Stengel decided to step down, which was thought to be the reason he turned down the opportunity to manage the Athletics the previous winter. UPI however, reported on June 1 that White Sox skipper Al Lopez was the likely successor to Stengel should 1960 be his final season. In the final year of a two-year contract, Casey maintained that he would make his decision at season's end, and that health would be a big factor.

The Yankees still only had a record of 20-20 on June 4, but went 23-5 over the next four weeks. Their four-game sweep of Chicago concluding on June 19 would move them into first place for the time being. Meanwhile, Maris was drawing raves for his performance in the first half of the season. Stengel himself said, "When we got this young man from Kansas City, I figured he was good. But I am ready to admit that Maris has been far more spectacular than I dared hope he would be."

Kansas City sportswriter Ernest Mehl wrote of Maris, " . . . he has been a spearhead of the Yankees, the one who has done more than any other to awaken the former champs and bring them back to strong contention for the title." Maris also was capturing the attention of his fellow major leaguers, who were responsible for selecting the All-Star teams. When the voting results were announced in early July, he received the highest number of votes among all major leaguers. It was observed that his home run pace at this time compared favorably to Babe Ruth's record-setting season of 1927. Maris insisted however, "I'm not thinking about the record. What I want most is for the Yankees to win the pennant."

On July 13 the Yankees hosted the second of the two All-Star games of 1960. Five Yanks saw playing time in the contest, including Maris, Mantle, Skowron, Berra, and Ford. The game was won by the Nationals 6-0, as Ford, who started, took the loss.

Having celebrated the 50th anniversary of his debut in organized pro baseball back in May, Stengel reached another milestone on July 30— his 70th birthday. The game that Saturday versus Kansas City at the Stadium was rained out, so a birthday ceremony was held the next day between games of a doubleheader. Old Casey was presented with many gifts at home plate, and the Kansas City team may have served as representatives from the city in which he was born back in 1890. Unfortunately, the Athletics had just beaten the Yanks in the first game 5-2 in eleven innings, and when a knife was handed to Stengel to cut the birthday cake, he pretended to slit his throat.

In early August, Maris suffered badly bruised ribs in a collision sliding into a base and missed 17 games. Thirty-five-year-old Berra, showing his versatility, replaced him in right field. Mantle was still being plagued by a bothersome right knee, but temporarily found himself in Stengel's dog house on August 14. In a game that day versus the Senators, he failed to run out a grounder in the sixth inning and was promptly yanked by Stengel. He sent Mantle to the clubhouse and reprimanded him harshly after the game. The next day, Mick responded by hitting two home runs to beat Baltimore 4-3, thereby vaulting New York back into first place.

The Yankee bullpen had been a weak spot, displaying a disturbing inconsistency over the first few months. In late July they sought help by acquiring veteran reliever Luis Arroyo from Jersey

There was no shortage of classic quotes from Stengel during the 1960 season. In June, pitcher Ralph Terry told him he would be unable to pitch that day due to twisting his knee while reading the paper. Stengel warned him "not to read anymore."

City of the International League. With a screwball and good control, he brought stability to the bullpen corps, and was unscored upon in 14 of his first 17 appearances. Seeking a left-handed bat off the bench, they also acquired veteran Dale Long from the Giants in late August for the $20,000 waiver price. In early September, they even inquired about the possibility of obtaining Dodger veteran Gil Hodges, though nothing materialized.

The Yankees entered September with a slim one-game lead over Baltimore, and had to overcome the upstart Orioles throughout much of the final month. Referred to as the "Baby Birds" or "Kiddie Korps," their starting line-up featured three rookies: Jim Gentile at first base, Marv Breeding at second, and Ron Hansen at shortstop, along with 23-year-old Brooks Robinson at third. In their starting rotation were Milt Pappas, Jack Fisher, and Steve Barber, all 21, and Chuck Estrada at 22.

The Yankees were scheduled to meet the Orioles in Baltimore for a crucial three-game series on September 2, 3, and 4. Going in one game up on the O's, New York would leave three days later two games behind. Pappas started off with a 5-0 three-hitter; Fisher took his turn with a 2-0 seven-hitter; and Estrada, with help from reliever Hoyt Wilhelm beat them 6-2 on five hits. A week-and-a-half later, with the teams tied for the top spot, they met for four games in New York, with rather different results. Ty Cobb was on hand for the entire series, having just returned from the Summer Olympics in Rome. He was photographed with Mantle, and was said to be giving the young superstar batting tips.

On September 18, the Yanks had put a serious dent in the Orioles' pennant hopes by completing a four-game sweep, now sitting four games up with just 11 left to play. The Orioles were destined for second place, which far exceeded anyone's expectations. It was their first season above .500, and from August 1 through September 17, they were never more than three games back.

New York just kept on winning, and with their ninth consecutive victory on September 25 behind the arm of young Ralph

Terry over the Red Sox in Boston, the franchise had captured their 25th AL pennant in the past 40 seasons. It was a somewhat unusual occurrence that the NL's pennant winner, Pittsburgh, would clinch on the same day. As the season wrapped up in October, the Yankees had won their final 15 games, and 19 of their last 21. Cobb called this pennant the masterpiece of Stengel's managerial career. Said the legend, " . . . he has already done more with less than any of the other years that I can recall that the Yankees won under his guidance." Stengel employed a great deal of platooning, a tactic he learned from the great John McGraw back in Casey's days with the New York Giants from 1921 through '23.

Like the Pirates in the NL, the Yankees led their league in runs scored as a team. Individually, Mantle led the loop in runs scored with 119, with Maris the runner-up with 98. It was somewhat unusual that the pennant winners had only one regular—Bill Skowron who had a batting average above .300—and their winningest pitcher, Art Ditmar, won only 15 games. Whitey Ford's 12 victories in 33 games pitched were the fewest he would ever win in a season in which he appeared in at least 25 games. Though no one pitcher stood out as the clear-cut ace, the staff as a whole was effective, tying Baltimore for the league lead in team ERA at 3.52. One of New York's most prominent statistical achievements was setting an AL record for home runs by a team in a season with 193.

The Yankees' road to their 25th Fall Classic was paved by quality pitching, power hitting, and the shrewd mind of Charles Dillon Stengel. The team was now poised to post many impressive individual World Series statistics, but would fall a tad short in one very important team category.

Chapter Sixteen

Bucs Defy the Numbers

In mid-October of 1960 in newsrooms across America, manual typewriters hammered out words like "fantastic," "implausible," and "weird" to describe the just-completed Pirates-Yankees World Series. Renowned sportswriter Fred Lieb, who had witnessed 47 Fall Classics wrote that it was "the wackiest ever played." It was believed that future historians would review the statistics and wonder "what happened?". The Yankees' individual statistical dominance was such that for the only time in the history of the World Series, the Most Valuable Player came from the losing team.

While the Yankees were regular visitors to World Series play over the previous several decades, lifelong Pirates fans as old as 35 had never known the excitement of watching their team in postseason play. The "Murderers Row" Yankees of 1927, featuring Ruth and Gehrig had dispatched Pittsburgh in four straight, and the drought began. The Pirates had actually won the Series two years before in 1925 against Walter Johnson's Washington Senators. Several members of that World Championship team were to be on hand for Game One at Forbes Field, including "Pie" Traynor and the team's

The official 1960 World Series programs published by the New York Yankees and Pittsburgh Pirates.

Pirates team captain Dick Groat at Forbes Field on October 4, the day before the start of the 1960 World Series. (National Baseball Library)

manager Bill McKechnie. Constructed in 1909, Forbes Field was the first modern-era steel and concrete ballpark. In its maiden season, the Pirates, led by Honus Wagner, went on to defeat Ty Cobb's Tigers in the '09 World Series.

The drama was set to begin at one o'clock on Wednesday afternoon, October 5 in Pittsburgh, the city of steel. Stengel was looking to capture his eighth world championship, which would surpass the seven earned by former Yankee pilot Joe McCarthy, and give him sole possession of the managerial record. The odds were placed at seven to five in favor of New York helping Stengel to achieve the milestone. The match-up of the two teams was generally billed as "Yankee power" versus "Pirate pitching," and many felt that New York's slugging ability plus its vast edge in series experience would prevail. Mantle expressed confidence in his ability to swing for the fences in Pittsburgh, noting that the outfield dimensions were not that different from Yankee Stadium. He recalled, "I played here twice before, and I hit one over the right field roof the first time." Mantle was referring to a blow that traveled more than 500 feet in an exhibition game in 1957, making him one of a small handful of hitters to reach that location.

With an overflow crowd of nearly 37,000 jammed into the cozy ballpark, the entire city was consumed by the Pirates' quest for their first world championship in 35 years. A local judge even delayed the start of a murder trial on the grounds that a jury might not be able to concentrate on the evidence due to the excitement of the Series. Even across the country, all but diehard Yankee fans seemed to be pulling for the "working class lunchpail hardhats" to emerge victorious over the "city slicker businessmen".

Pregame ceremonies included Pennsylvania Governor David Lawrence throwing out the first pitch to veteran catcher Smoky Burgess, and Pittsburgh native Billy Eckstine singing the national anthem to the accompaniment of the University of Pittsburgh Band.

Each team would be sending its winningest pitcher to the mound in the opener as two tall right-handers, Vern Law and Art

Ditmar would oppose each other. According to Bucs manager Murtaugh, Law had fully recovered from the mild ankle sprain he suffered a few days before. Murtaugh also had shortstop Groat back in his familiar number-two slot in the order. While he was not certain Groat would be able to perform at 100 percent so soon, he said, "I've never seen anyone with greater determination. Were it anyone except Dick, I might have my doubts."

After the opening festivities were complete, Yankee shortstop Tony Kubek led off by singling sharply off the third-base bag. He was quickly erased when Hector Lopez bounced into a double play, bringing Maris to the plate for his World Series debut. He promptly delivered a Law offering deep into the right field upper deck for a quick 1-0 New York lead. It didn't stand long, however, as Pittsburgh came right back in the bottom of the first, sending Ditmar to an early shower. Bill Virdon led off with a walk, and when he attempted a delayed steal, caught Kubek off guard. Berra threw down to second, but with no one to cover the bag, the throw sailed into center, and Virdon scampered to third. Kubek convinced the official scorer later that due to his negligence in failing to cover, the error belonged to him rather than Yogi. Groat then doubled into the right-field corner, bringing home Virdon with the tying run. Skinner singled, scoring Groat, and after Dick Stuart lined out, Clemente singled to score Skinner. Before Ditmar could even record the second out, Stengel went to the bullpen to bring in Jim Coates, who retired the two batters he faced. With one inning in the books, Pittsburgh held a 3-1 lead.

The Yankees thought they had something going in the top of the second when Berra led off with a single and Bill Skowron followed with another. In a rather unusual move, Stengel sent veteran left-handed hitter Dale Long up to pinch-hit for third baseman Clete Boyer with no outs in the second, but the strategy failed as Long flied to right with no advancement of the runners. Bobby Richardson then lined to Skinner in left, who then doubled Berra off second to quell the rally.

The bespectacled Virdon made what was likely the play of the game off of Berra in the Yankee fourth. Maris reached safely again in his second at-bat, singling to right center, and Mantle then walked, which brought up Berra with nobody out. Yogi launched a 410-foot fly to deep right center field which both Virdon and Clemente pursued. Though they collided slightly, Virdon managed to come up with a spectacular one-handed catch, getting spiked by Clemente in the process. Murtaugh said afterwards, "Yogi whaled the daylights out of that ball, but Bill got us out of a big inning." Virdon added, "It was not my greatest catch, but it was certainly the most enjoyable." The Yankees did score one that inning on a Skowron single, and Pittsburgh held a slim 3-2 lead going into the bottom of the fourth.

The Pirates then came to bat, and with one down, Don Hoak was issued a walk from Coates. Mazeroski then came up, having been struck out by Coates in his first at-bat in the second inning. Here in the fourth Maz was challenged with the first two pitches over the heart of the plate, and found himself in the hole 0-2. Maz said later that he thought Coates would waste one in this situation but came in with a letter-high fastball that he pulled over the left-field wall for what would later become the second-most famous home run of his entire career. It was also the first homer he had hit at Forbes Field since July 16. Pittsburgh now held a 5-2 advantage, and though the scoring wasn't finished, they would not relinquish the lead.

The Pirates added a run in the sixth when Virdon doubled off the right-field screen scoring Mazeroski. In the Yankee eighth, Law gave up singles to the first two batters, then gave way to ace reliever Roy Face. The forkball specialist then struck out Mantle and induced Berra to fly out. Murtaugh went out to the mound and told Face to strike out Skowron, which is exactly what he did to get out of trouble. New York staged a rally in the top of the ninth as Gil McDougald started it off by singling to right. Stengel then inserted Elston Howard as a pinch-hitter for reliever Ryne Duren, and the catcher slugged a two-run homer into the right field seats. Tony Kubek followed with a single, but was forced at second on a Richardson grounder, and Hector Lopez came up representing the tying run. Face got him to ground to Maz who started the 4-6-3 double play to preserve the 6-4 win for Law and the Pirates.

Rain throughout the morning the next day in Pittsburgh threatened Game Two, however it cleared up about 15 minutes before game time. New York was poised to go out and put on a two-game display of the vaunted Yankee power.

The pitching match-up featured New York's Bob Turley, 9-3 during the season, opposed by Pittsburgh's 18-game winner Bob Friend. The Yanks drew first blood in the third with a single by Kubek that scored Richardson and a double by McDougald that brought Kubek across. Both teams scored one run in the fourth, and at 3-1, that was as close as it would get. Mantle slugged a two-run homer in the fifth, and the floodgates burst wide open in the sixth as New York now led 12-1. The Yankees sent 12 men to the plate that inning, with Howard and Richardson each hitting safely twice. The next inning, Mantle cracked another home run, a three-run shot over the center field wall that measured 478 feet. They added yet another run in the ninth as it ended in a romp, 16-3. The Pirates' 13 runners left on base was one shy of a World Series record. The Yankees' 16 runs was the second-highest total for a series game, behind only the 18 scored by their forefathers in Game Two of 1936. As for his two home runs, Mantle said after the game, "I wish I could have saved them for a time when they meant something. Homers don't mean much in a 16-3 game."

The teams took a day off and traveled to New York for Game Three on October 8. Just a couple of the noteworthy dignitaries among the 70,000 in Yankee Stadium that Saturday afternoon were former president Herbert Hoover and India's Prime Minister Nehru. Cardinal broadcaster Joe Garagiola would point out to Berra the next day that the popular longtime Yankee had become such a world figure that he drew more applause when announced than Hoover or Nehru. Yogi replied, "Sure, I'm a better hitter."

Yankees Southpaw Whitey Ford ended his 1960 season in fine form, hurling two shutouts in the '60 Series.

Part of the Game Three pregame events included Lucy Monroe singing the Star-Spangled Banner accompanied by the 69th Veterans Band, and recently retired Ted Williams throwing out the ceremonial first pitch to Elston Howard. Murtaugh, celebrating his 43rd birthday would be sending veteran Vinegar Bend Mizell to the hill to oppose Yanks lefty Whitey Ford, who was setting a series record with his 13th start. In the top of the first, Ford set the Pirates down in order, and the Yankees then picked up where they had left off in Game Two. Mizell was gone after one-third of an inning with one run in and the bases full. Former Brooklyn Dodger Clem Labine came in for Pittsburgh and merely threw gas on the fire. The first batter he faced, catcher Howard, beat out a slow roller up the third-base line to score Mantle. Then 166 lb. Bobby Richardson, who had only one home run in 1960 hit a grand slam just inside the left-field foul pole. One out later, the Pirates brought in their third pitcher of the game, lefty Fred Green, and they would go into the second inning down 6-0.

Pittsburgh didn't reach base until Virdon's double to lead off the fourth, and he was stranded at second as the inning ended. Then in the bottom half of the fourth, New York had another big inning to put the game out of reach. Mantle hit a two-run shot into the left field bullpen, his third homer of the series, and Richardson stroked a two-run single. With only seven RBI after the All-Star break, Richardson, the unlikliest hero, had set a World Series record with six RBI in one game.

Ford was masterful for New York on the mound, scattering only four hits. Aside from the one walk he issued to Gino Cimoli in the seventh, he only went to a count of three balls on two other batters. It would not be a happy birthday for the Bucs skipper, and with the 10-0 drubbing, New York had outscored Pittsburgh 26-3 in the previous two games.

The Pirates were able to come back with their ace Law the next day, Sunday, October 9, as Stengel sent young righty Ralph Terry. Law worked out of a bases-loaded jam in the first, and the game remained scoreless until the bottom of the fourth. With two outs, Yankee first baseman Moose Skowron hit a solo home run into the right field stands. The Bucs came right back in the next inning as Law helped his own cause with an RBI double. Virdon added a single that drove in two as Pittsburgh took a 3-1 lead. Law got into a bit of trouble in the seventh as Richardson's fielder's-choice grounder scored Skowron. With runners on first and second and only one out, Murtaugh summoned Roy Face from the bullpen

Casey Stengel posed with Mickey Mantle in 1956, after Mantle had captured the AL Triple Crown.

to preserve the slim 3-2 lead. The first batter he faced, Bob Cerv, hit the ball 400 feet to right center, but a spectacular leaping catch was made by Virdon. Face then got Kubek to bounce back to the mound to end the inning, and the lead remained intact. The little forkballer hurled the final 2 2/3 innings, not allowing the Yankees a hit, and saving the victory for Law. Aside from Face's great relief work, Mantle credited Pirates center fielder Virdon and his stellar defensive play in Games One and Four with keeping Pittsburgh in the series. When reporters went into the Yankee locker room after the game, they found most members of the team watching the New York Giants—Pittsburgh football game.

Knotted up at two games apiece, Game Five was to be the final series game at Yankee Stadium for 1960. Stengel went back to his Game One starter Ditmar, and again the Yanks' winningest pitcher of the season exited early. He didn't survive the second inning, giving up three hits and three runs in that frame, although two were unearned due to a costly error by McDougald. The big blow was a Mazeroski double down the left field line that scored both Burgess and Hoak. Down 3-0 going into the bottom of the second, New York got on the board on a Kubek ground out that scored Howard. Pittsburgh came right back with an RBI single by Clemente off reliever Luis Arroyo, and Stengel then brought in Bill Stafford. Maris slugged a towering solo homer into the third deck in right field off of Pirates lefty Harvey Haddix in the third inning, and the score would remain 4-2 until the top of the ninth. Young Stafford went five innings without giving up a run, and Stengel was reportedly furious at himself for not starting him over Ditmar. The team's most effective starter during the season, Ditmar's performance in the '60 Series was a bitter disappointment.

With one out in the seventh, Haddix gave up back-to-back singles, and Murtaugh again went to Face. Just as he did the day before, Face hurled 2 2/3 innings relief. Before the game, Face had sent a World Series program over to the Yankee clubhouse to be autographed, and it came back without a single signature. Some wondered if this had given him the extra incentive to bear down a little harder.

With Hoak adding an RBI single in the ninth, the game ended 5-2 with the Pirates now heading back home with a three games-to-two edge. The Series resumed on October 12, and the 38,580 that filled Forbes Field was the largest crowd of the four games that would be played there. Bob Friend took the mound for the Pirates, Ford for New York, though he didn't know he was starting until two hours before game time. When Ford drove in Berra with an infield single in the first, it was actually all New York needed, though they would tack on many, many more. Friend was pulled before the first out of the third inning was recorded, having hit a batter, then giving up three straight hits. He was charged with five earned runs in his brief outing, and his series performances were nearly as disappointing to Pittsburgh as Ditmar's was to New York. The Yankees continued to pile it on, adding two runs each in the sixth, seventh, and eighth innings. Ford meanwhile, pitched most of the game with a blister on his finger, yet never allowed a runner past second base. He gave up a total of seven hits in the 12-0 shellacking for his second complete-game shutout of the series, and he had done it on just three days' rest. Richardson continued his torrid hitting with three more RBI, which established a still-standing World Series record of 12 for one series. Kubek chipped in on his 24th birthday by scoring two runs. Remarkably, in the three games that Pittsburgh lost, they were outscored 38-3.

Now, the outcome of this most unusual 1960 World Series came down to one day, one game, and subsequently one inning. Murtaugh had no doubt that Law, winner of Games One and Four would be his starter in the finale. "All I want from Vern today is five good innings. If he can give me that I'll have Face and Friend ready," said the Bucs skipper. Stengel was less definitive about his choice of starter, reserving the right to change his mind at game time. He was leaning towards Bob Turley, but also named Stafford, Bobby Shantz, and Ralph Terry as possibilities, in that order. A couple of hours before the first pitch was to be thrown, Turley went to his locker and found a brand new ball tucked inside one of his baseball spikes, indicating to him that he would be getting the nod.

Law set the Yankees down in order to open the game, and after retiring the first two batters in the bottom half, Turley walked Skinner. First baseman Rocky Nelson then put Pittsburgh on the board with a home run into the right field stands to the sheer joy of the Forbes Field crowd. After a one-two-three Yankee second inning, Turley gave up a lead off single to Burgess, and out came Stengel with the quick hook. Not wanting to let things get out of hand, he brought in the 21-year-old Stafford, who pitched five innings of scoreless relief in Game Five. He proceeded to load the bases, but then got Law to hit into a double play that forced Burgess at home. Virdon, however, slashed a single to right center, scoring both Hoak and Mazeroski for a 4-0 lead.

New York broke into the scoring column with Skowron's opposite-field home run off Law to lead off the fifth inning. They came right back in the sixth, driving Law from the game and taking a 5-4 lead. After Richardson had opened the sixth with a single and Kubek walked, Murtaugh brought Face in from the bullpen. With one out, Mantle came through with an RBI single, and Berra smacked a tremendous three-run home run down the right field line that landed in the second deck.

Going into the top of the eighth with Face still pitching for Pittsburgh, the Yanks still clung to a 5-4 lead. Face retired the first two batters, Mantle and Maris, but then found himself in more trouble. He walked Berra, allowed an infield single to Skowron, and gave up a single to back-up catcher John Blanchard that scored Berra. Clete Boyer then doubled into the left field corner scoring Skowron before the third out was finally recorded. Things looked bleak for Pittsburgh, trailing 7-4 going into the bottom of the eighth. At this time, cases of champagne were being moved into the Yankee clubhouse in anticipation of a victory celebration.

The chain of events that transpired over the next inning and a half were truly remarkable. The hand of fate intervened and inexorably altered what many believed was a logical conclusion. Pirates third baseman Hoak, a hard-nosed ex-middleweight boxer had delivered a highly spirited pep talk in the dugout an inning earlier, and the team was poised to make the kind of comeback they had made so many times that season. Pinch-hitting for Face, Gino Cimoli opened the bottom of the eighth inning with a single to right center. Virdon hit what at first appeared to be a perfect double-play ball to Kubek at shortstop, but possibly hitting a pebble, it took a freakish hop, skipped up and struck him in the throat. Kubek collapsed in a heap and was down for several minutes as the runners were safe at first and second. It was feared at first that he may have a fractured larynx, and despite his protests, Stengel removed him

Pandemonium has broken out at Forbes Field as Bill Mazeroski is just about to make his Series-ending home run official. (National Baseball Library)

from the game in favor of Johnny DeMaestri. Speaking of the incident later, Kubek stated that he didn't have a chance on the play. "It happened so quickly that I couldn't even raise my glove in self-defense."

The fateful play, which should have left Pittsburgh with two out and no one on base opened the flood gates for a five-run inning. Groat then singled to left, scoring Cimoli, bringing Jim Coates on to pitch for New York. The first out of the inning was recorded when Skinner sacrificed, moving the base runners up to second and third. Rocky Nelson flied out to shallow right for out number two as the runners were unable to advance. Clemente stepped into the batter's box, and what was about to occur was as pivotal a play as there would be, previous to the stunning conclusion. He bounced a slow chopper down to Skowron at first, and inexplicably, pitcher Coates failed to cover the bag for the putout. Instead of ending the inning with New York up 7-6, Pittsburgh, had runners on first and third. Up came back-up catcher Hal Smith, who had replaced Burgess behind the plate in the top of the eighth. Smith had been discarded by the Yankees while still in their minor league system in 1954, and had contributed to many Pirate victories with his bat this season. He rose to the occasion in this clutch situation, magnifying Coates' defensive mistake by smacking a three-run homer over the left field wall for a 9-7 lead.

Pittsburgh brought in Friend to start the ninth and hopefully finish it off, but the Yankees would not go down easily. After giving up singles to the first two batters, Richardson and pinch hitter Long, Friend was quickly pulled and lefty Haddix brought in. Haddix got Maris to foul out, but Mantle singled in Richardson with Long stopping at third. Berra then drilled a sharp grounder down the first-base line to Nelson that very well could have been a Series-ending double play. Nelson fielded it cleanly and ran a few steps over to step on first. He turned, likely assuming he would be able to throw down to second to double up Mantle, but found him just a few feet away from first. Nelson lunged to tag Mantle, but Mickey managed to slide back into first, avoiding the tag. McDougald was allowed to score on the play, tying the game at nine. Some speculated later that if regular first baseman Dick Stuart had been in at the time, he likely would not have been able to handle the grounder at all. Skowron then grounded out to end the inning, and the stage was now set for the most dramatic bottom of the ninth in Series history.

A few most unusual, perhaps untimely occurrences had brought it all down to this classic situation. A bizarre bad hop on a grounder to shortstop that wiped out a likely double play; an almost unforgivable mental error by an experienced pitcher failing to routinely cover first base; a narrowly missed tag in the top of the ninth that made the bottom half of the ninth even necessary.

Just-turned 24-year-old Bill Mazeroski, son of a coal miner, stepped up to the plate to lead off the fateful ninth inning and answer destiny's call. Though decades later, many historians and analysts would continue to hail him as likely the greatest defensive second baseman to ever play the game, it is this one magical moment with his bat that he will most often be associated. After taking Ralph Terry's first pitch for a ball, Mazeroski drove the second offering, a high fastball, up and over left fielder Yogi Berra's head and into the trees behind the ivy-covered wall. The jubilant young man danced around the bases, waving his batting helmet around in his hand, as fans spilled out of the Forbes Field stands to form a welcoming committee. As he came around third base, home plate umpire Bill Jackowski desperately tried to hold back players so Maz could touch home and make it official before being mobbed. At that instant, the city of Pittsburgh went berserk. Ticker tape and even phone books were tossed out of office building windows; traffic was stopped at intersections as horns honked and ecstatic fans paraded amidst the debris. The town was reveling in its first world championship in 35 years. Arthur Daley of the *New York Times* wrote, "This was New Year's Eve, the Mardi Gras, and Armistice Day jammed into one boisterous package." A champagne-soaked Mazeroski declared in the winner's clubhouse, "I'm too happy to think." Dejected Yank pitcher Terry offered, "I don't know what the pitch was. All I know is it was the wrong one." Berra, no stranger to postseason excitement, including catching Don Larsen's perfect game in 1956 admitted that this was the most exciting game he ever played. Frank Gibbons of the *Cleveland Press* wrote, "The last game may not have been baseball at its best, but it was baseball at its most exciting; the kind of game that keeps alive the tradition that is the national pastime." Jimmy Powers of the *New York Daily News* reck-

The batting helmet and bronzed bat used by Pirates second baseman Bill Mazeroski when he hit his famous World Series home run shown here as they are displayed at the Baseball Hall of Fame. (Courtesy, National Baseball Hall of Fame and Museum)

oned, "It was a win for the poor little guys against the big rich guys swollen with past loot and overladen with records."

Pirate outfielder Gino Cimoli observed, "They set the records, but we won the game." The Yankees had set a series record with a team batting average of .338 while Pittsburgh batted just .256. New York had outscored them 55-27, with a team ERA of 3.54 compared to the Bucs' lofty 7.11. Individually, little second baseman Richardson set a still-standing record of 12 RBI, and remains the only World Series MVP to be selected from the losing team. *Sports Illustrated* referred to him after as "the mouse that roared." The Corvette he was presented with, however, was quickly traded in for a station wagon. Berra established new series records for most World Series (11), Series games (68), and RBI (36), to go along with adding to his records for at-bats (245), hits (68), total bases (111), as well as several fielding records.

Add to this the lack of contribution from several Pirate regulars; left fielder Bob Skinner missed five of the seven games with an injury; slugging first baseman Stuart had zero RBI in 20 at-bats; 18-game winner Friend was 0-2 with a 13.50 ERA.

Whether or not it was supernatural forces at work, divine intervention, or perhaps blatant favoritism from Lady Luck, the Pirates managed to render many impressive statistics virtually meaningless.

Chapter Seventeen

Shake-up in the Bronx

It was back on October 12, 1948 that Yankee general manager George Weiss surprised the baseball world and was ridiculed in the process by hiring Casey Stengel to replace the recently departed Bucky Harris. In his 22 seasons as a major league manager, Harris had taken his teams to the World Series three times. Stengel, on the other hand, had never finished higher than fifth place in his nine seasons spent with the Dodgers and Braves. Stengel had stepped in to take over a team that had finished a disappointing third place in 1948, and commenced to reel off an unprecedented and still unequaled five consecutive world championships. The success didn't stop there as Stengel took his squad back to the Fall Classic five more times over the next seven seasons. Many believed that taking the 1960 edition into the postseason was one of his more impressive feats as manager. The team had come out of Spring Training with less than great expectations and got off to a shaky start. They came on strong, fought off the upstart Orioles late, and did it all with a less-than-dominating pitching staff. By winning his tenth pennant as manager, Stengel had tied the legendary John McGraw,

Five days after the conclusion of the 1960 World Series, it was announced that Stengel would not return as manager. Let go largely due to his age, Stengel said at the time, "I'll never make the mistake of turning 70 again."

for whom he had formerly played, for the all-time major league lead.

In the season of 1960, Stengel was working on the final year of a two-year contract. In May he told reporters that he would decide after the season if he would continue to manage, citing health as a major factor in his decision. Spending a week in the hospital due to a viral infection in early June and turning 70 years old on July 30 fueled further speculation that his days of managing the Yankees might be numbered.

New York ultimately made their way to their 25th World Series appearance, and after its startling conclusion, the fates of Stengel and G.M. Weiss were said to be the team owner's number-one priority. Stengel was not commenting on his future plans, saying he would come to a decision later in October.

Five days after the seventh game of the '60 World Series, Yankee owners Topping and Webb made the decision for him. That day a press conference was held at the Hilton Savoy in New York City, where it was announced that Stengel would not return to the helm of the Yankees. Topping believed that 70 was just too old to handle the enormous strain of managing in New York where a winner was expected every year. Stengel's illness during the season convinced them that the change was inevitable. Topping later revealed that the change would have been made even if the Yankees had won the World Series in four straight games. Writer Dan Daniel backed this up by claiming he had been leaked word of the firing just days before the beginning of the Series. Daniel also wrote that Stengel could have the job of managing the new NL New York team that would be starting up in 1962. This would appear to be the first suggestion in print of Stengel's future involvement with the Mets franchise.

Stengel displayed bitterness towards Topping, and made it clear to reporters after that as far as he was concerned he was fired, not retired. Either way, he certainly would not suffer financially, receiving a severance package that included a payment of $160,000 as part of a profit-sharing plan set up by Larry MacPhail many years before.

The day after Stengel's dismissal, New York baseball writers sponsored a lavish dinner at the Waldorf-Astoria to honor him, giving a proper sendoff. Certainly the writers were sorry to see him go, having been provided with countless colorful quotes over the years. When George Weiss was paying tribute to Stengel at the farewell dinner, he became very emotional, which was something that the writers were very unaccustomed to seeing from the stoic G.M. Perhaps he was struck with the realization that the end of his tenure as the organization's top baseball man was near as well.

With Topping and Webb making known their desire to enforce a 65-year age limit, the 66-year-old Weiss officially resigned from his position two weeks later on November 2. The future Hall of Fame executive announced that he felt it was time to take it easy, and he would now act as a consultant for the team. Though he would be drawing a $50,000 salary, his new position bore virtually no defined duties or responsibilities. Weiss' departure was truly the end of an era as he was the last link to the Jacob Ruppert-Ed Barrow regime of the 1930s.

The Yankees were now in the hands of two longtime employees of the team, with Ralph Houk moving into the manager's office, and Roy Hamey, who had worked for them for 19 years hired as the new G.M.

Most seemed to believe that Stengel's days in the game were not over. Bill Veeck said, "Baseball just can't afford to lose a man like Casey Stengel," and said that he could have a job in the White Sox organization if he so desired. Some speculated that he might end up with the vacant Giants managerial job. On November 14, new Tigers owner John Fetzer, along with front office executives Jim Campbell and Rick Ferrell visited Stengel at his Glendale, California home. They attempted to persuade him to take over as the team's skipper, and even offered a front office position as an alternative, but Stengel wouldn't commit. He reportedly asked for three weeks to think it over, but apparently the Detroit brass wasn't prepared to wait, hiring Bob Scheffing one week later.

In mid-December, Stengel was given first choice to become the first manager in the history of the American League's new Los Angeles franchise, but the most he would do was advise their new G.M. on player acquisitions. The final offer of the year that he received came from the brand new owner of the Kansas City Athletics just before Christmas. Stengel was given the opportunity to take an executive position back in the city of his birth, but he declined. In little more than a year, both Stengel and Weiss would take over a New York Mets team that made Kansas City look like a pennant contender by comparison.

As for the New York Yankees, the changes in management appeared to have a positive effect, as they remained the team to beat in the American League for the next several years.

Chapter Eighteen

Handing out the Hardware

With the 1960 baseball campaign now in the books and the shock of the dramatic World Series setting in, the time had come for rewarding the top performers in various aspects of the game. In keeping with the rather unusual nature of the season itself, there were several peculiarities and interesting sidebars to the stories of the recipients of such awards.

With the Pittsburgh Pirates officially wearing the crown as World Champions of baseball, accolades were due to numerous individuals throughout the major leagues for special achievement.

The envelope please . . .

National League Most Valuable Player:

Dick Groat. On November 17, an employee of the Jesop Steel Company of Washington, Pennsylvania received a telephone call informing him that he had just won the National League Most Valuable Player Award for 1960. Dick Groat had done what he had routinely done each year: finished his summertime job and went to his wintertime job.

Groat had been an All-American in both baseball and basketball at Duke University, and led the nation in scoring on the court in his senior year in 1952. He signed with the Pirates for a $75,000 bonus and made his major league debut three days after graduation without having spent a day in the minors. After his rookie season with Pittsburgh, Groat entered the National Basketball Association as a guard with the Fort Wayne Pistons. He spent 1953 and '54 in the service, and after his discharge, Branch Rickey convinced him that playing both basketball and baseball full time would wear him down, and that he should focus strictly on baseball.

By 1960, Groat was the team's captain, the leader of the infield, an outstanding hit-and-run man, and the best number-two hitter in the league. By mid-season, Warren Spahn said that Groat was the player the Pirates could least afford to lose. By August, Dick Young was hailing him as a strong MVP candidate. Voters agreed, and he captured the award in a landslide. He became the first Pirate to win the award since its inception in 1931, and broke Ernie Banks' string of two consecutive MVP awards.

The voting results:

Dick Groat	Pitt	276 pts.
Don Hoak	Pitt	162
Willie Mays	S.F.	155
Ernie Banks	Chi	100
L. McDaniel	St.L.	95
Ken Boyer	St.L.	80
Vern Law	Pitt	80
R. Clemente	Pitt	62
E. Broglio	St.L.	58

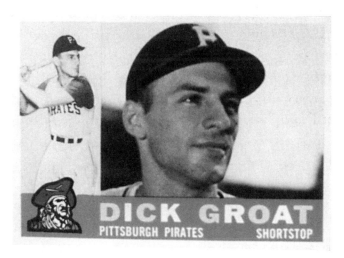

Dick Groat certainly earned his $18,000 salary for 1960 as the NL's MVP. Not only had he been a basketball star at Duke University, he was the roommate of Richard Nixon's brother Ed. (Courtesy Topps Inc.)

E. Mathews	Mil	52
Hank Aaron	Mil	49
Elroy Face	Pitt	47
Del Crandall	Mil	31
Warren Spahn	Mil	27
Norm Larker	L.A.	21
Stan Musial	St.L.	18
Maury Wills	L.A.	7
Vada Pinson	Cin.	6
Joe Adcock	Mil	5
S. Burgess	Pitt	2
F. Robinson	Cin	2
Larry Sherry	L.A.	2
P. Herrera	Phi	1

American League Most Valuable Player:

Roger Maris. Voting results for the AL MVP were considerably closer than in the NL, with Maris barely edging out teammate Mickey Mantle. Maris's 39 home runs and 112 RBI were certainly worthy of recognition, but many felt that it was Mantle's award to win, as he actually received ten first-place votes to Maris's eight. Casey Stengel himself supported Mickey, and upon his dismissal predicted he would win it, saying, "Who stands out ahead of him?" At the end of the season, Stengel praised Mantle for his heart, saying he had played on an ailing right knee that would have put most players out of action. Still others felt that Mantle wasn't deserving because he didn't play up to his full potential. Voters may have also credited the Yankees' addition of Maris in '60 to their rise to pennant winners from third place in '59.

In light of Maris and Groat winning the MVP Awards in their respective leagues for 1960, it is worth reflecting that these

1960 Topps baseball card # 377. With his trade to the Yankees before the '60 season, Roger Maris was set to embark on a nine-season span in which he went to the World Series seven times. In this season, he would earn the first of two consecutive MVP Awards. (Courtesy Topps Inc.)

two were very nearly traded for each other at the winter meetings in December of 1959. The proposed trade between Kansas City and Pittsburgh, which would have included a few additional players was agreed to in principal, but when Pirate G.M. Joe Brown had one night to think it over, he changed his mind. It is impossible to predict how this trade may have affected the balance of power, or what trade the Yankees may have made if they hadn't acquired Maris.

The voting results:

Roger Mari	N.Y.	225 pts.
Mickey Mantle	N.Y.	222
Brooks Robinson	Balt	211
Minnie Minoso	Chi	141
Ron Hansen	Balt	110
Al Smith	Chi	73
Roy Sievers	Chi	58
Earl Battey	Wash	57
Bill Skowron	N.Y	56
Jim Lemon	Wash	36
Tony Kubek	N.Y.	29
Chuck Estrada	Balt	28
Ted Williams	Bos	25
Vic Wertz	Bos	22
Yogi Berra	N.Y.	21
Jim Gentile	Balt	21
Pete Runnels	Bos	18
Nellie Fox	Chi	11
Vic Power	Cle	11
Steve Barber	Balt	7
Luis Aparicio	Chi	6
Jim Perry	Cle	6
Gerry Staley	Chi	4
Jim Bunning	Det	3

Gene Woodling	Balt	3
Harvey Kuenn	Cle	3
Bud Daley	K.C.	3
Mike Fornieles	Bos	2
Charley Maxwell	Det	2
Jimmie Piersall	Cle	2

Cy Young Award:

Vern Law. As the ace of the pitching staff of the World Champion Pirates with 20 wins and no other pitcher who truly stood out above the rest, Law would seem to have been the odds-on favorite choice going in. A little luck may have increased his victory total further, as two of his losses were by a score of 2-1, and one by a score of 3-2.

Created in 1956 by Commissioner Ford Frick, the honor was only bestowed upon one pitcher per year rather than one in each league. By the fall of '60, many voting members of the BBWAA were calling for the award to be presented in each league, and in an editorial, *The Sporting News* wholeheartedly agreed. Frick refused to budge on the issue, and it wasn't until 1967, two years after he left office, that one pitcher in each league would be awarded. It was speculated in the encyclopedia *Total Baseball* that if two Cy Young awards had been given in 1960, Baltimore's 22-year-old rookie Chuck Estrada likely would have been the AL recipient.

National League Rookie of the Year:

Frank Howard, outfield, Los Angeles Dodgers. A former standout in basketball at Ohio State, the 6'7" behemoth had slugged a total of 82 home runs and drove in 253 RBI in the previous two seasons in the minor leagues. He began the 1960 season back in Spokane, but was recalled by the Dodgers on May 12, having bat-

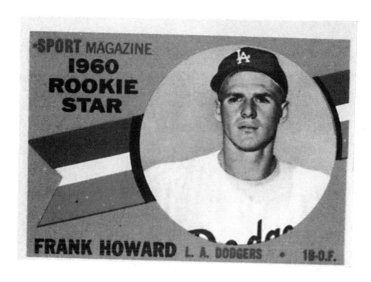

Frank Howard's 1960 Topps baseball card # 132. Big Frank came into the world weighing 13 lbs., 6 oz. By 1960 he wore a size 50 sportscoat with only a 34" waist, and swung a bat as heavy as 45 oz. He told Pee Wee Reese on a television show that when he goes home to Columbus, Ohio, his mother bakes him a nice big raccoon. "Mighty fine eating," he said. (Courtesy Topps Inc.)

ted .385 over the first month. In order to bring up Howard, the Dodgers waived longtime right fielder Carl Furillo, effectively ending his noteworthy big league career.

Howard debuted with L.A. that season on May 13, and in his fourth game with the team he hit a grand slam in the eighth inning to beat the Braves in Milwaukee. Braves manager Charlie Dressen would say he had seen only one player who combined Howard's strength and quickness: Babe Ruth. About a week later on May 25, the Dodgers were at Forbes Field in Pittsburgh where 25 years earlier to the day, Ruth hit his final home run, a tremendous blast. This day, the 23-year-old Howard hit an estimated 565-foot home run that helped beat Pittsburgh 5-1.

Howard's prodigious power began to elicit further flattering comments. Former Dodger Pete Reiser said, "In my 26 years in baseball, I've never seen anyone hit the ball like Howard, and remember, I saw Ralph Kiner when he came up, and Hank Greenberg in his prime." L.A. writer Melvin Durslag wrote, "If Howard continues to attack the baseball as he has during his latest engagement in the major leagues, a lot of lives may be endangered."

Big Frank appeared in 117 games in '60, hit 23 home runs, had 117 RBI, and batted .268. With only 22 ballots cast in the NL Rookie of the Year poll, Howard received 12. Pancho Herrera of the Phillies was second with four, followed by Philadelphia pitcher Art Mahaffey (three), Ron Santo (two), and fellow Dodger Tommy Davis (one).

American League Rookie of the Year:

Ron Hansen, shortstop, Baltimore. In the Spring of 1957 while in the Cubs organization, Hansen suffered a ruptured spinal disc and was given only a 40% chance of ever playing baseball again. By 1960 he had rehabilitated from the injury and was given the opportunity to become the Orioles' starting shortstop. Observers began to sit up and take notice, and in mid-May Joe King referred to him in print as "the eye-catcher in the East . . . does everything well and commands attention." He also compared the 6'4" Hansen to former Cardinals outstanding shortstop Marty Marion. Hansen played all but one of Baltimore's games in 1960, slugging 22 home runs and driving in 86. Defensively, he led all major league shortstops in putouts with 325.

Hansen joined the Army Reserves for a six-month stint just a few weeks after the season ended (not a common choice for young players in these days), and learned of his selection as the AL's top freshman while in basic training. Nearly a unanimous winner, Hansen received 22 of the 24 votes cast. Teammates Chuck Estrada and Jim Gentile received one vote apiece.

National League Batting Title (Silver Bat Award):

Dick Groat. In his march toward the batting crown, Groat had four or more hits in a game eight times in '60, including a six-for-six game against Milwaukee on May 13. A couple of months after the season, Al Dark commented on how much he admired Groat for coming back in late September and risking his batting title when his wrist wasn't fully healed. Dark added, "When he told me he was going to play, I even advised him against it, but he insisted he wanted to win it going away—and he did."

American League Batting Title:

Pete Runnels, Boston Red Sox. Despite battling painful stomach ulcers, the second baseman captured the AL title with a .320 average, marking the first time this century that the batting champs of both leagues finished with averages below .330. Another oddity was that both Runnels and Groat had season totals of two home runs in 1960. Runnels also went on to win the AL title in 1962.

Gold Glove Award:

Sponsored by the Rawlings Sporting Goods Company, the award was created in 1957 to reward the best defensive player at each position. That first season, the award was given out to only one player at each position, regardless of league. The following year it was expanded to honor one player at each position in each league. At that time it was the players themselves who selected the winners, though they could not vote for any player on their own team.

National League:

1B	Bill White	St. Louis
2B	Bill Mazeroski	Pittsburgh
SS	Ernie Banks	Chicago
3B	Ken Boyer	St. Louis
LF	Wally Moon	Los Angeles
CF	Willie Mays	San Francisco
RF	Hank Aaron	Milwaukee
C	Del Crandall	Milwaukee
P	Harvey Haddix	Pittsburgh

American League:

1B	Vic Power	Cleveland
2B	Nellie Fox	Chicago
SS	Luis Aparicio	Chicago
3B	Brooks Robinson	Baltimore
LF	Minnie Minoso	Chicago
CF	Jim Landis	Chicago
RF	Roger Maris	New York
C	Earl Battey	Washington
P	Bobby Shantz	New York

Sporting News Fireman of the Year Award:

With the importance of the role of relief pitchers having grown considerably over the years, *Sporting News* editor J.G. Taylor Spink decided it was finally time to recognize this overlooked group of players. On July 22, 1960, the publication announced the creation of the Fireman of the Year award, with the trophy featuring a statue of a pitcher wearing a fireman's hat. The concept of the award was universally hailed throughout baseball as all seemed to appreciate the importance of bullpen specialists in the game. Frick commended *The Sporting News* on its decision; BBWAA president Edgar Munzel said "This fills a definite void in baseball's list of Oscars;" and Joe Cronin stated, "The important contributions made by relief pitchers is something of which the individual clubs have been aware of for some time, but the leagues have never taken any official recognition of it. Therefore this is a very splendid thing Mr. Spink is doing."

The method created for selecting the recipients, which was the predecessor to the "Rolaids Relief Man Award" was a rather simplistic point system. One point was awarded for each save, and one point for each win in relief.

National League:

Lindy McDaniel—St. Louis

American League:

Mike Fornieles—Boston:

Sporting News Major League All-Star Team:

Before the 1960 World Series, *The Sporting News* polled 294 members of the BBWAA as they did annually to determine the best players in the majors at each position, including three pitchers.

The results:
1B   Bill Skowron
2B   Bill Mazeroski
SS   Ernie Banks
3B   Eddie Mathews

LF	Minnie Minoso
CF	Willie Mays
RF	Roger Maris
C	Del Crandall
P	Vern Law
P	Warren Spahn
P	Ernie Broglio

Sporting News All-Rookie Team:

The Baltimore Orioles appeared to have a very bright future with five of the 12 selections. With an excellent crop of candidates overall, those selected included:

1B	Jim Gentile	Baltimore
2B	Marv Breeding	Baltimore
SS	Ron Hansen	Baltimore
3B	Ron Santo	Chicago
LF	Frank Howard	Los Angeles
CF	Tommy Davis	Los Angeles
RF	Ken Walter	Philadelphia
C	Jim Pagliaroni	Pittsburgh
P	Chuck Estarada	Baltimore
P	Steve Barber	Baltimore
P	Fred Green	Pittsburgh
Utility	Frank Herrera	Philadelphia

Sporting News Major League Manager of the Year:

Danny Murtaugh, Pittsburgh. In his four stints as Pirates manager, which totaled 15 seasons, Murtaugh led the team to two pennants and four other division crowns. In the end, however, it was the 1960 edition's .617 winning percentage that was his best.

Sporting News Executive of the Year

George Weiss. Though New York lost the '60 World Series, Weiss received some measure of personal satisfaction by being honored as the majors' top front-office man. He faded from the Yankee scene three weeks after the series ended, but resurfaced the following year as the G.M. of the newly formed Mets. Weiss played a big role in assembling their championship team of 1969.

Chapter Nineteen

AL Gives Birth to Twins (Senators and Angels)

When the proposed Continental League officially ceased operations in early August, adding new franchises to both the American and National Leagues now appeared a foregone conclusion. There had been no really strong support for expansion until the CL came along with the intention of occupying many of the top minor league cities.

Now, several of those cities had assembled formidable ownership groups and were lobbying for inclusion. Upon its demise, the CL had been promised that four of their cities would be absorbed into the majors. NL owners had already unanimously voted at their meeting on July 18 that if the third league concept did not come to fruition in the very near future, it would expand its membership to ten teams. On August 30, with the CL now out of the picture, the AL announced that it, too, would add two new teams no later than December 1961.

New York appeared destined for a future NL franchise to replace the departed Dodgers and Giants. It was believed that they could utilize Yankee Stadium until the proposed facility in Flushing Meadow was completed. Yankee co-owners Dan Topping and Del

Webb insisted that AL expansion should include Los Angeles, since New York would be giving up territorial rights to the NL for a new team there, and the Dodgers should do the same. Commissioner Frick agreed with the Yankee owners and felt that the L.A. area was easily capable of supporting two major league teams. Houston was also thought to be a prime location for expansion, and with the country's seventh-highest population, it was the largest city without a major league team. Plans to build a domed stadium in the city were revealed on August 20. Another Texas location, the Dallas-Fort Worth area was pushing hard for an expansion team as well. A site had been selected in Arlington, midway between the two cities where another domed stadium was being considered. With 1.6 million people in the metropolitan area and financing apparently in place, this seemed a viable major league location. Representatives of the area met with members of the AL and NL expansion committees in L.A. in early September to present their bid. Still other cities applying for consideration were Minneapolis-St. Paul, San Diego, and Toronto.

Members of the AL expansion committee included Yankees co-owner Webb, George Medinger of the Indians; Joseph Inglehart, Orioles; and Hank Greenberg of the White Sox. The NL committee consisted of the Dodgers' Walter O'Malley, Bob Carpenter, Phillies; John Galbreath, Pirates; and Lou Perini, Braves. Perini had made suggestions regarding how expansion teams might stock their rosters. He envisioned new teams blending old-time names such as Red Schoendienst, Alvin Dark, Stan Musial, and Ted Williams with young players. Said Perini, "Can you imagine how a Williams would draw if he wore a New York uniform for a year?" Greenberg and Bill Veeck favored a plan that had been discussed earlier whereby one team would be added to each league creating two nine-team leagues, necessitating inter-league play. Veeck said that his father, William Sr., who had owned the Cubs decades earlier had first proposed inter-league play back in 1922. Bill DeWitt of the Tigers thought the AL should immediately add four teams.

The game was entering uncharted territory with the expansion debacle taking many twists and turns and months to resolve. *The Sporting News* editorialized in its September 21 issue, "Major League Baseball in the midst of expansion talk could well study and learn some lessons from the orderly fashion in which the NFL is expanding under the direction of Commissioner Pete Rozelle." Much to the chagrin of Commissioner Frick, the process turned out to be anything but orderly. Galbreath of the Pirates said that a commitment had been made to take in four of the CL's cities and that the NL had intended to honor that. An unnamed AL official claimed that their league was not necessarily committed to selecting former CL cities. There was no shortage of disagreement on where new teams should be placed. NL president Giles said that there was no guarantee that his league would grant New York a franchise. He added, "Actually, there are two schools of thought on the subject. One group favors New York, and the other favors cities that have never been in the majors." By October, one AL group headed by Greenberg was campaigning hard for a west coast team. Another AL faction wanted to grab both Houston and Dallas-Fort Worth, creating a natural rivalry.

Finally, at an historic meeting at the Sheraton-Blackstone Hotel in Chicago on October 17, 1960, NL owners voted unanimously to add New York and Houston to their circuit beginning in 1962. It appeared that the NL had beaten the AL to the punch again by grabbing the Texas territory first, just as it had moved into California three years before. The expansion committees of the two leagues were scheduled to meet several weeks prior, but only Cronin showed up from the AL. The NL saw this as a lack of good faith and proceeded on its own. The AL however, would make headlines of its own a week-and-a-half later.

The setting was the Savoy-Hilton Hotel in New York, where on October 26, the American League magnates dropped a bomb on the baseball world. The league voted to add two new teams that would begin playing in April of 1961—less than six months away!

Los Angeles gained a unanimous vote from the AL owners to join the fold, and along with Chicago became baseball's only two-team cities. Many observers felt that AL owners were motivated by revenge against the NL and Dodgers owner O'Malley, who was seen as the culprit for claiming California first and also snatching Houston away from their grasp. Cronin solidly supported the L.A. expansion effort, which would become a serious bone of contention between the two leagues. He also told reporters before the meeting that his league was "further advanced and better prepared for expansion than the NL."

An equally important aspect of the AL proceedings was that the Washington Senators, the team that had represented the nation's capital for 60 seasons was approved for transfer to the Minneapolis-St. Paul area. The other new franchise was granted to Washington D.C. to immediately replace the departing Senators, as it was nearly unfathomable to most that the capital could be left without big league baseball. One official confided that the Senators transfer simply would not have been approved without the replacement team. Senators owner Calvin Griffith, who had taken over the team upon the death of his foster father Clark in 1955 had discussed the possibility of relocating them for the past three years. The city of Washington had broken ground on a $23-million baseball stadium on July 8 of 1960, but Griffith, with a move in mind, was dragging his feet on signing a lease.

In mid-October, longtime Washington baseball writer Shirley Povich wrote that rumors persisted that the Senators would move to Minneapolis. Griffith responded, "That's a lot of baloney . . . . It's news to me that the AL would discuss transferring the Washington team elsewhere. I appreciate the future we have here." He also pointed out that the team had their most successful season in years both on the field and at the gate. Roughly a week later, Griffith was on his way to Minnesota.

The city of Minneapolis, which had just lost its NBA Lakers to Los Angeles was prepared to immediately begin expanding

Metropolitan Stadium from a capacity of 22,000 up to 40,000. City officials also promised Griffith a guaranteed yearly attendance of nearly one million; increased radio and television money; profits from concessions; and a low stadium rental fee. Many years later, during a speech at a rotary club in Minnesota in 1978, Griffith caused a bit of a stir when he revealed what may have motivated him to leave Washington. He said, "Black people don't go to ballgames, but they fill up a 'rassling' ring and put up such a chant they'll scare you to death. We came to Minnesota because you've got good hard-working white people here."

They were one of the original American League franchises and the only team the legendary Walter Johnson had hurled for. It was for them that the phrase was coined "Washington—first in war, first in peace, and last in the American League!" The Senators were leaving just as their fortunes on the field appeared to be improving. They had finished dead last the previous three seasons, and in 1960 made a serious run at a spot in the first division. By the beginning of September, the underdog Senators had surged into fourth place and not only created enthusiasm in Washington, but had been adopted by many fans outside the D.C. area. Manager Cookie Lavagetto was considered a "miracle man" and was thought to be a legitimate candidate for manager of the year. Also, attendance had increased by 128,000 in '60 to slightly over 743,000.

The 4,768 who attended the Senators' final game of the season at Griffith Stadium on October 2 had no way of knowing it was to be the team's swan song in the capital.

American League owners were jubilant at beating the NL at fielding two new teams. Cronin called their plan, which also called for an increase in the schedule to 162 games "the most forward-looking and progressive program in baseball history." Many members of the baseball press however, were less than impressed with the AL's hasty plan. Jimmy Powers of the *New York Daily* News referred to adding two new teams instantly as "watering the whiskey." Bob Burnes of the *St. Louis Globe-Democrat* wrote that the AL would be

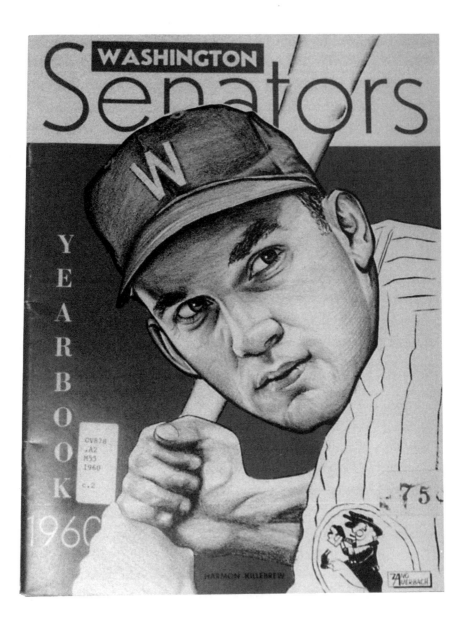

The final yearbook published by the original Washington Senators in their final season in the nation's capital, which featured future Hall of Famer Harmon Killebrew on its cover. After 60 seasons in D.C., they would now go by the name "Minnesota Twins".

wise to postpone expansion until 1962. Melvin Durslag of the *L.A. Examiner* wondered if the AL didn't get caught up in the drama of expansion with its sudden rush to add teams. Dick Young, as he often would, put an interesting slant on the decision by calling it one of spite, led by Del Webb. Young wrote that Webb and O'Malley had been friends, and it was assumed that Webb's construction company would get the contract to build Dodger Stadium which didn't happen.

Commissioner Frick himself was a bit perturbed over the AL's decision to start up in '61, preferring '62 like the NL. He met with Giles and Cronin on November 1 and cautioned the leagues to act in harmony in the future regarding expansion plans. Frick decreed that there would be no more surprise expansions, and that the two leagues would meet and decide together when and where the next teams would be created.

Many offers were coming in from groups seeking ownership of the new franchises. One member of a group bidding for the Washington team was vice-president Richard Nixon. Hank Greenberg, V.P. of the White Sox, was preferred by many AL owners to head the Los Angeles ownership group. Greenberg let it be known that he would seek a two-year lease on the L.A. Coliseum for the team, sharing the facility with the Dodgers for 1961. Bill Veeck was also thought to be considering divesting himself of the White Sox and bidding on the L.A. team.

While Frick had originally supported the idea of the AL moving into L.A., he seemed to do an about face in mid-November. At an AL meeting in New York on November 16, he informed the owners of a seemingly forgotten rule that required a unanimous vote from major league owners to allow a team to enter the territory of an existing team. While O'Malley was not opposed to sharing Dodger Stadium with the new L.A. team when it opened in 1962, he was much less interested in being co-tenants with them at the Coliseum in '61. Rule 1(c), as it was known would put the L.A. expansion effort in serious jeopardy, and many AL owners were seeking to have it amended in order for their plans to move forward. In the meantime, at an AL meeting on November 17, the Washington franchise was awarded to a group headed by retired Air Force general Ellwood "Pete" Quesada. The chairman of the Federal Aviation Agency, Quesada was a World War II hero and longtime friend of Cronin, Tom Yawkey, and Cal Griffith. Reportedly, Griffith had tipped off Quesada on the Senators' move as early as the summer of '60, suggesting that he bid on a possible replacement team. After being awarded the D.C. team, Quesada wasted no time with management appointments. In less than 24 hours he had tabbed Ed Doherty as general manager and Mickey Vernon as field manager. Vernon had been a very popular player for the old Senators, having spent 13 of his 20 seasons with the team.

Cronin announced on November 22 that it was still the AL's intention to start up in L.A. in '61, but also offered an alternative plan. The two nine-team leagues plan with inter-league play concept was revived. The AL suggested that if the NL would start up in Houston in '61, they would proceed with only Washington, withholding L.A. until '62. New York would also be added to the NL in '62, completing the two ten-team leagues.

Baseball's winter meetings were to be held in St. Louis from December 5-7, where a resolution of the expansion issue was imperative. *The Sporting News* editorialized that the major leagues were at a crossroad, and urgently needed the wisdom, patience, and unselfishness to adequately solve its problems. It had been a turbulent year for the game, and Frick was facing the most serious challenge of his reign as commissioner.

Working into the wee hours of the morning on December 6, a compromise was reached that allowed L.A. to join the AL in 1961. The NL couldn't agree on the nine-team setup, partly because they felt it would not be possible to have Houston operating by '61. The resolution included the new L.A. owners paying the Dodgers an indemnity fee of $450,000. They would also play their home games of '61 at L.A.'s Wrigley Field, former home of the Pacific Coast League's Angels. Once all of the details were ironed out, O'Malley credited Frick with strong leadership, and stated, "The Commissioner steered a straight course. If he had lost his sense of direction, we would have wound up in an awful mess." Frick himself credited Pirates owner Galbreath as a key negotiator, recognizing him for his significant role in helping to reach a compromise. O'Malley displayed a measure of class after the meetings concluded when he instructed his staff to assist the new L.A. team with any aspect of organizing that they might need.

Since Hank Greenberg had backed out of the ownership picture of the new L.A. franchise, it was awarded on December 6 to a group headed by Gene Autry. A huge box-office draw as a singing cowboy in Hollywood movies in the 1930s, Autry still received thousands of fan letters each month. Many in Los Angeles felt that the AL couldn't have picked more highly respected business and civic leaders than Autry and partner Bob Reynolds. Their ownership of L.A. radio station KMPC may have been a factor in their desire to acquire another baseball franchise for the area. In the first two seasons the Dodgers were in L.A., O'Malley had their games broadcast over KMPC. After the '59 season, O'Malley abruptly shifted the games to competing station KFI. When the opportunity came along to move into O'Malley's territory and assure themselves of baseball broadcasts, which were a valuable commodity, Autry and Reynolds moved quickly.

The new team immediately hired Fred Haney as its first general manager. Haney had piloted the Milwaukee Braves to the world championship in 1957, and in a return engagement with the Yankees the following year, held a 3-1 advantage before losing in seven. Autry also visited Casey Stengel at this time and tried to convince him to manage in L.A. Said Autry of the experience, "After four hours of 'Stengelese,' I was more confused than ever." In the end, Stengel told him he'd let him know in three weeks, but Autry simply couldn't wait. On December 12, they announced the hiring of Bill Rigney as manager. Rigney had just been fired as manager of the Giants six months earlier.

It was suggested to Autry that the new team be nicknamed "Champions" after his famous horse. He felt that it may take a few years before they reached champion status, and opted to retain the "Angels" name that had been used by L.A.'s minor league team for many years. Quesada had announced at the winter meetings in St. Louis that the D.C. team would retain the name "Senators," respecting Washington's long association with big league ball. As for the relocated Senators, Griffith decided in early December on the name "Twins," signifying Minneapolis and St. Paul as the "twin cities". Their park, Metropolitan Stadium was equidistant between the downtown areas of the two towns. Most observers felt that Minnesota would do extremely well at the gate, and getting an established team with stars on the roster helped immensely.

The draft to stock the rosters of the two new teams was originally scheduled for November 28; however, the dispute between the leagues would set it back until the resolution came in early December. At the AL meeting on November 17, the owners devised the plan the teams would follow. Each of the eight AL teams would make 15 players available off of their 40-man roster, and would lose seven in the draft. The new teams would pick ten pitchers, two catchers, six infielders, and four outfielders, with no positional restriction on the remaining six picks. A $75,000 fee would be paid for each selection. They would also have the right to select one player from each team's farm system for a price of $25,000.

When the list of available players was made public, Bill Shea, one of the principals in bringing an NL team to New York, voiced his displeasure. He stated that if similar quality players were offered in the NL draft the following year, they would simply not be accepted. This is rather amusing in light of how the New York Metropolitans fared in their early years, becoming the very model of expansion ineptitude.

The historic first expansion draft took place on December 14, 1960, at the American League office in Boston. Los Angeles won the coin toss to determine which team would pick first and made Yankee pitcher Eli Grba their first choice, as well as the answer to a trivia question in the process. When the draft had concluded, the list of selections by the new franchises included:

Los Angeles

Pitchers: Eli Grba (New York), Duke Maas (New York), Jerry Casale (Boston), Fred Newman (Boston), Truman "Tex" Clevenger (Minnesota), Bob Sprout (Detroit), Aubrey Gatewood (Detroit), Ken McBride (Chicago), Ron Mostler, (Baltimore), Dean Chance (Baltimore), Bob Davis (Kansas City), Ned Garver (Kansas City).

Catchers: Ed Sadowski (Boston), Bob Rodgers (Detroit), Bob Wilson (Cleveland).

Infielders: Eddie Yost (Detroit), Ken Aspromonte (Cleveland), Gene Leek (Cleveland), Ken Hamlin (Kansas City), Jim Fregosi (Boston), Ted Kluszewski (Chicago), Don Ross (Baltimore), Julio Becquer (Minnesota), Steve Bilko (Detroit).

Outfielders: Bob Cerv (New York), Ken Hunt (New York), Jim McAnany (Chicago), Faye Throneberry (Minnesota), Albie Pearson (Baltimore).

Washington

Pitchers: Bobby Shantz (New York), Dave Sisler (Detroit), Pete Burnside (Detroit), Johnny Klippstein (Cleveland), Carl Mathias (Cleveland), Dick Donovan (Chicago), Ed Hobaugh (Chicago), Hal Woodeshick (Minnesota), Hector Maestri (Minnesota), Rudy Hernandez (Minnesota), Joe McClain (Minnesota), Tom Sturdivant (Boston).

Catchers: Pete Daley (Kansas City), Dutch Dotterer (Kansas City), Gene Green (Baltimore), Heywood Sullivan (Boston).

Infielders: Coot Veal (Detroit), Dale Long (New York), Marion Zipfel (New York), Jim Mahoney (Boston), Bob Johnson (Kansas City), Chester Boak (Kansas City), Billy Klaus (Baltimore), Lee Burke (Baltimore), Johnny Shaive (Minnesota).

Outfielders: Willie Tasby (Boston), Gene Woodling (Baltimore), Chuck Hinton (Baltimore), Marty Keough (Cleveland), Jim King (Cleveland), Joe Hicks (Chicago).

The baseball press for the most part was not terribly optimistic that the new teams would field competitive squads right away. Sam Greene of the *Detroit News* wrote, "We are facing a period in which the quality of baseball will be the worst since the war years." Dick Young predicted the new teams wouldn't win 40 games apiece. Sid Ziff of the *L.A. Mirror-News* said that although the pickings were slim, the AL had not yet scraped the bottom of the barrel. "After all," he wrote, "they didn't bring back Satchel Paige!"

For better or for worse, there was now no turning back as the expansion era had officially begun. Robert Burnes of the *St. Louis Globe-Democrat* had penned earlier, "Strange isn't it, how many people have come out strong for expansion, but no one could blueprint it until Branch Rickey forced baseball's hand." For the innovative, forward-thinking Rickey, the addition of new major league teams turned out to be the final contribution on an extraordinary resume.

Chapter Twenty

Reflections of a Year
for the Ages

In reviewing the major leagues of the twentieth century, the end of the year of 1960 could in many ways be thought of as a dividing line between the so-called "good old days" and the dawning of a new era. Change had been affected in so many aspects of the sport, as beginnings and endings of some sort were nearly a weekly happening, seemingly littering the landscape. Changes were occurring in several teams' ownership situations, the cities that would host major league teams, the stadiums in which they would play, the amount of games that would be played, and the very structure of the leagues themselves.

The concept of brand new teams being created and operating within the realm of major league baseball was a story that lasted literally throughout the entire year. It is incalculable to determine how the proposed Continental League, if it had come to fruition, would have altered the course of baseball history. As it was, even in failing, it directly led to the addition of two American League teams in 1961, two in the National in '62, and charted a new direction for the game. Longtime minor league cities such as Minneapolis and Houston were soon to be elevated to major league status. Part of the package included an increase in the season schedule from the traditional 154 games up to 162. The increase immediately paved the way for the Yankees' Roger Maris to surpass Babe Ruth's legendary and hallowed 60 home run figure. There is little doubt that an executive decision in the fall of '60 to expand the schedule helped to subsequently relegate Babe to the number-two position on the single-season home run list for more than three and a half decades.

Though the historic expansion of '61-'62 wasn't the abysmal failure that many predicted, it only encouraged the further dilution of the product that came later in the decade.

The watershed year of 1960 was simply rife with significant beginnings and endings. It was considered the end of an era in Chicago when Chuck Comiskey resigned as White Sox vice-president on June 8. The grandson of Hall of Famer and team founder Charles Comiskey, it marked the first time in the team's 60-year history that there was no Comiskey in its front office. The Detroit Tigers experienced a new beginning when radio and television executive John Fetzer, who had owned a small part of the team, purchased controlling interest in October. Today, a wing at the Baseball Hall of Fame is named in his honor due to his generous contributions.

With the death of Kansas City Athletics owner Arnold Johnson in March, the fate of that team was up in the air for virtually all the duration of the year. Johnson had purchased the franchise from the Mack family in 1954 for 2.8 million dollars and immediately transferred it to Kansas City. His death had now created an ongoing legal problem for his widow, as several potential ownership groups surfaced periodically. Two weeks after Johnson's passing, a group of New Jersey businessmen announced that they had made a substantial offer to buy the Athletics and move them to that state. Former Cardinals shortstop Marty Marion was part of a group of investors looking to purchase the team and transfer them to Houston. Wealthy Miami businessman Bill MacDonald planned to buy them and move them to Minnesota. By the end of the season, the Kansas City fans had rallied enough to reach the 850,000 attendance figure that would prevent the franchise from leaving the city at this time. Meetings were being held in a Kansas City probate court to straighten out the ownership situation, and a deal was finally reached on December 19. Forty-two-year-old Charles O. Finley, a Chicago insurance tycoon, assumed control by purchasing 52% of the team for $1,975,000. He had outbid a local Kansas City group who had offered $1,850,000.

Finley, a former batboy with Birmingham of the Southern Association, had been attempting to buy a big-league team for seven years. Ironically, he made an effort to buy the Athletics back in 1954, but was outbid by Johnson. He had also tried to buy the Tigers, but was beaten out by Fetzer, and had an option to buy 54% of the White Sox if Veeck and Greenberg ended up with the new L.A. franchise. Finley felt that the Athletics' availability represented his last chance to land a team and was going to go all out to do it, even if it meant bidding as high as 2.5 million.

At the press conference to announce his purchase, Finley stressed that he would take a backseat in the operation of the team. In reviewing his 20-year ownership of the franchise, it doesn't appear he adhered to that particular philosophy.

There were several comings and goings with regard to the land on which the ballplayers trod in the performance of their duties. The year witnessed the demolition of Brooklyn's classic and beloved Ebbets Field, while a short time later three thousand miles away, ground was broken in Los Angeles on a new home for the Dodgers. The franchise that moved west with the Dodgers, San Francisco, had left behind their temporary home, Seals Stadium, and christened a brand new Candlestick Park in the Spring of '60. The state-of-the-art facility would serve the Giants for the rest of the century—a full 40 seasons.

By year's end it became official that two more parks would be joining the circuit as showcases for major league baseball. Metropolitan Stadium in Minnesota was now the new home of the relocated Senators, while Wrigley Field in Los Angeles was to be the playground of Angels. And Griffith Stadium would be the one constant bridging the gap between the old and new Senators for one year as construction began in July of '60 on the D.C. team's future home. The Tigers saw a change in the park in which they played, but a change in name only. Their home field was dropping its longtime name of "Briggs Stadium" in favor of "Tiger Stadium," the moniker it would carry for the rest of its existence.

Not only did the year feature significant changes, but innovations came about that took hold in certain specific aspects of performance and evaluation. Baltimore Orioles manager Paul Richards had witnessed his catchers set an AL record in 1959 with a total of 49 passed balls, with 38 coming while knuckleballer Hoyt Wilhelm was on the mound. After only one month of the '60 campaign the figure had reached 14—11 of which came on the fluttering, hard-to-predict pitches of Wilhelm. In early May, catcher Gus Triandos set an AL record with three in one inning, and totaled four in that particular game. Richards had an idea, realizing that the official rule book stated that there was no restriction on the size of a catcher's mitt. He had the Wilson Sporting Goods Company manufacture a mitt that was a full one-and-a-half times the size of the standard glove, to be used only when Wilhelm pitched.

On May 27, Orioles catcher Clint Courtney used the mitt for the first time in a game, and in Wilhelm's nine innings pitched that day there were no passed balls. The concept was a complete success, and by early July after Wilhelm had pitched 51 1/3 innings with his catchers using the mitt there had been only one passed ball. Richards' innovation became commonplace within a short time as standard equipment used to catch knucklers.

Identifying the need to better evaluate the performance of relief pitchers, Chicago baseball writer Jerome Holtzman created a specific criteria to define the "save". This was adopted by *The Sporting News* in '60, and led to the save becoming an official statistic in 1969.

Cincinnati Reds relief pitcher Jim Brosnan authored a rather ground-breaking baseball book that was released in the Spring of

1960 called *The Long Season*. Extremely articulate and a very competent writer, Brosnan took a behind-the-scenes look at the game from a major leaguer's perspective, and he ruffled a few feathers in the process. Many insiders felt the journal was just a little too revealing.

The year was certainly not without controversies or unpleasant incidents. On August 15 with the Braves playing at Cincinnati, future Hall of Famers Eddie Mathews and Frank Robinson engaged in a violent fist fight during a game. During the seventh inning of the first game of a doubleheader, Robinson slid hard, trying to stretch a double into a triple. After Mathews tagged him, words were exchanged, and a flurry of punches soon followed. Robinson was clearly on the losing end with a bloody nose and swollen eye.

A far more serious incident had occurred on August 4 in Chicago as future manager Billy Martin, with the Reds at this time, charged the mound and attacked Cubs rookie pitcher Jim Brewer after nearly being beaned. Martin landed a blow that broke the orbit bone under the right eye of the young pitcher, requiring immediate surgery. Martin was subsequently fined $500 and given a five-day suspension. In a move that was unprecedented in the majors, the Cubs and Brewer filed a lawsuit seeking $1,040,000 in damages. The case ultimately took nine years to settle, and in the end, Martin had to pay $10,000 in damages and $12,000 in legal fees.

Jimmie Piersall, referred to by midsummer as the only true eccentric player left in the game, was involved in a series of incidents. Some were concerned that his behavior was a little too similar to his actions back in 1952, which were chronicled in the book and subsequent movie *Fear Strikes Out*. Some of his Cleveland teammates felt his actions were hurting their pennant chances, and umpires were disgusted with him. During a game on July 23 versus Boston, Ted Williams was at bat when Piersall started doing what appeared to be an Indian war dance in center field. A short time later while on suspension he was seen during a game playing football and basketball in the bullpen. Opposing players had taken to calling the colorful character "Flaky" or "Squirrel". Piersall's saving grace was that he was still a productive hitter and an exceptional center fielder.

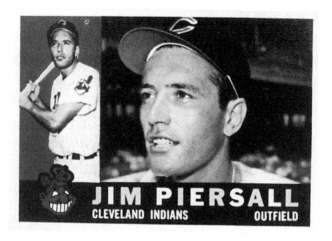

Jimmie Piersall's 1960 Topps baseball card # 159. The outfielder was continually making news with his oftentimes bizarre behavior. In August of '60 he was quoted as saying, "I wouldn't have an umpire's job, mainly because of guys like me." (Courtesy, Topps Inc.)

Another colorful individual from a generation before still had a place in the game as a broadcaster. Hall of Fame pitcher Dizzy Dean, former Cardinals legend of the 1930s was teamed with Pee Wee Reese on the CBS television Game of the Week. Dean regularly entertained viewers with his unorthodox use of the English language. Before an Indians-Red Sox game that was televised on June 17th of '60, Harvey Kuenn was presented with the Silver Bat Award for having won the AL batting title in 1959. Dean later informed the viewers " . . . Harvey Kuenn got a gold and silver bat or somethin' for sometin' or other he did."

A situation was developing in baseball in the Summer of '60 that involved international politics. Because of the unsettled political climate on the island of Cuba, the International League team that had played there since 1954 was pulled out in mid-season. League president Frank Shaughnessy announced on July 7 that the Havana Sugar Kings would be playing the remainder of their home schedule in Jersey City, New Jersey due to increasingly strained relations between U.S. and Cuba, hoping to avoid incident. With the transfer officially approved at a league meeting on July 13, the primary objective was the protection of American players. Havana played its first game in Jersey City at Roosevelt Stadium on July 15. In September, Commissioner Frick ordered American players to stay out of Cuba, foregoing involvement in the island's winter leagues. The door to organized professional baseball in the United States for Cuban players was beginning to close.

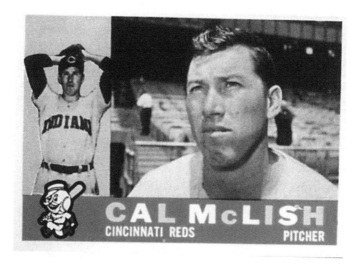

Cal McLish's 1960 Topps baseball card # 110. The Cincinnati pitcher had a record of 4-14 in 1960, but what was most unusual was his birth certificate, which read "Calvin Coolidge Julius Caesar Tuskahoma McLish". (Courtesy, Topps Inc.)

The game witnessed the stirring comeback in 1960 of master batsman Ted Williams, as he exited in truly grand fashion. Ever the showman, he possessed the dramatic flair and the wisdom to depart as they were still cheering. There were many observers who believed that he could have maintained his ability to hit for a couple more seasons. His NL counterpart, Stan Musial, also atoned for an uncharacteristically mediocre '59 season. In '60, he improved on virtually every offensive category from the year before and showed that he wasn't quite ready to leave the game.

In addition, another veteran outfielder bounced back from a lackluster '59 season. After being cast off by the Phillies, whom he had played for 11 seasons, Richie Ashburn rewarded the Cubs by leading the NL in on-base percentage and bases on balls in his first season with the team. Eddie Yost, the Tigers' third baseman in his 16th big-league season reached an impressive milestone this season. On August 2 he surpassed Pirates great third baseman Harold "Pie" Traynor with his 1,865th game played at the position—more than any third sacker in history.

So many fine performances, so many legends and legends in the making, baseball's popularity was seemingly at an all-time high. The National League set a new record for attendance in '60 at 10,684,963, surpassing the previous record set in 1947 by roughly 300,000. The Dodgers topped the '57 Braves for the NL team record, and four other major league teams set attendance marks of their own, including the Giants, Pirates, White Sox, and Orioles.

The major leagues had the opportunity to showcase their talents and further increase baseball's popularity internationally in the fall of '60. Two days after the conclusion of the World Series, the San Francisco Giants left for a couple of exhibition games in Hawaii, and from there engaged in a 16-game tour of Japan. During this exhibition series, Willie McCovey slugged at a tremendous clip and became the rave of Japanese newspapers, television, and magazines. Willie Mays greatly enjoyed his time in Japan, and upon leaving said, "I'll be taking home many cherished memories. The

Japanese were very warm hearted, and it was a rewarding experience." Many noted how improved the Japanese players were, and the Giants very nearly signed several to contracts. Baseball officials from the U.S., and Japan even discussed the possibility of a "World's Series" between the two countries in the coming years.

One need to look no further than *The Sporting News*, in its 75th year of publication in '60, as an indication of baseball's stature within the sports world. At that time, even in the dead of the off-season, a typical issue of 36 pages in length would contain roughly 26 pages of baseball coverage.

By the fall of 1960, football was beginning to make inroads in terms of popularity and exposure, as the professional game was branching out to new locations. The NFL brought the Dallas Cowboys aboard in '60, and the Minnesota Vikings in '61, with both franchises going on to achieve considerable success both on the field and at the gate. The American Football League and its eight new teams also kicked off its inaugural season in September of 1960, creating even further competition for the sports fan's dollar, and vying for the television viewer's attention.

Early November of 1960 witnessed the election of John Kennedy as President of the United States, bringing about a new era for the nation. A portion of a line from his inauguration speech a couple of months later could have also applied to the end of 1960 from a baseball standpoint: " . . . symbolizing and end as well as a beginning—signifying renewal as well as change."

Truly, the torch had been passed, from old era to new. The positively unique year of 1960 was left for baseball fans to fondly recall, and for historians to dissect, analyze, and even shake their heads in wonder.

Appendix A

1960 League Standings and Statistics

National League

	W	L	Pct.	G.B.
Pittsburgh	95	59	.617	-
Milwaukee	88	66	.571	7
St. Louis	86	68	.558	9
Los Angeles	82	72	.532	13
San Francisco	79	75	.513	16
Cincinnati	67	87	.435	28
Chicago	60	94	.390	35
Philadelphia	59	95	.383	36

American League

	W	L	Pct.	G.B.
New York	97	57	.630	-
Baltimore	89	65	.578	8
Chicago	87	67	.565	10
Cleveland	76	78	.494	21
Washington	73	81	.474	24
Detroit	71	83	.461	26
Boston	65	89	.422	32
Kansas City	58	96	.377	39

Batting and Pitching Leaders

National League

Batting Average:

Dick Groat	Pit	.325
Norm Larker	L.A.	.323
Willie Mays	S.F.	.319
Roberto Clemente	Pit.	.314
Ken Boyer	St. Louis	.304

Home Runs:

Ernie Banks	Chi.	41
Hank Aaron	Mil.	40
Eddie Mathews	Mil.	39
Ken Boyer	St. Louis	32
Frank Robinson	Cin.	31

Runs Batted In:

Hank Aaron	Mil.	126
Eddie Mathews	Mil.	124
Ernie Banks	Chi	117
Willie Mays	S.F.	103
Ken Boyer	St. Louis	97

Runs Scored:

Bill Bruton	Mil.	112
Eddie Mathews	Mil.	106
Vada Pinson	Cin.	107
Willie Mays	S.F.	107
Hank Aaron	Mil.	102

Doubles:

Vada Pinson	Cin.	37
Orlando Cepeda	S.F.	36
Bob Skinner	Pit.	33
Frank Robinson	Cin.	33
Ernie Banks	Chi	32

Triples:

Bill Bruton	Mil.	13
Vada Pinson	Cin.	12
Willie Mays	S.F.	12
Hank Aaron	Mil.	11

(3 players tied with 10)

Slugging Percentage:

Frank Robinson	Cin.	.595
Hank Aaron	Mil.	.566
Ken Boyer	St. Louis	.562
Willie Mays	S.F.	.555
Ernie Banks	Chi.	.554

On-Base Percentage:

Richie Ashburn	Chi.	.416
Frank Robinson	Cin.	.413
Eddie Mathews	Mil.	.401
Wally Moon	L.A.	.387
Willie Mays	S.F.	.386

Bases on Balls:

Richie Ashburn	Chi.	116
Eddie Mathews	Mil.	111
Jim Gilliam	L.A.	96
Frank Robinson	Cin.	82
Darly Spencer	St. Louis	81

Stolen Bases:

Maury Wills	L.A.	50
Vada Pinson	Cin.	32
Tony Taylor	Chi., Phi.	26
Willie Mays	S.F.	25
Bill Bruton	Mil.	22

Pitchers

Wins:

Warren Spahn	Mil.	21
Ernie Broglio	St. Louis	21
Vern Law	Pit.	20
Lew Burdette	Mil.	19
	(3 tied with 18)	

Earned Run Average:

Mike McCormick	S.F.	2.70
Ernie Broglio	St. Louis	2.75
Don Drysdale	L.A.	2.84
Stan Williams	L.A.	3.00
Bob Friend	Pit.	3.00

Strikeouts:

Don Drysdale	L.A.	246
Sandy Koufax	L.A.	197
Sam Jones	S.F.	190
Ernie Broglio	St. Louis	188
Bob Friend	Pit.	183

Winning Percentage:

Ernie Broglio	St. Louis	.700
Vern Law	Pit.	.690
Warren Spahn	Mil.	.677
Bob Buhl	Mil.	.640
Bob Purkey	Cin.	.607

Shutouts:

Jack Sanford	S.F.	6
Don Drysdale	L.A.	5
	(5 tied with 4)	

Complete Games:

Warren Spahn	Mil.	18
Vern Law	Pit.	18
Lew Burdette	Mil.	18
Glen Hobbie	Chi.	16
Bob Friend	Pit.	16

Appearances:

Roy Face	Pit.	68
Lindy McDaniel	St. Louis	65
Don Elston	Chi.	60
Dick Farrell	Phi.	59
Ed Roebuck	L.A.	58

Innings Pitched:

Larry Jackson	St. Louis	282
Bob Friend	Pit.	276
Lew Burdette	Mil.	276
Vern Law	Pit.	272
Don Drysdale	L.A.	269

Saves:

Lindy McDaniel	St. Louis	26
Roy Face	Pit.	24
Bill Henry	Cin	17
Jim Brosnan	Cin	12

American League

Batting Average:

Pete Runnels	Bos.	.320
Al Smith	Chi.	.315
Minnie Minoso	Chi.	.311
Bil Skowron	N.Y.	.309
Harvey Kuenn	Cle.	.308

Home Runs:

Mickey Mantle	N.Y.	40
Roger Maris	N.Y.	39
Jim Lemon	Was.	38
Rocky Colavito	Det.	35
Harmon Killebrew	Was.	31

Runs Batted In:

Roger Maris	N.Y.	112
Minnie Minoso	Chi.	105
Vic Wertz	Bos.	103
Jim Lemon	Was.	100
Jim Gentile	Balt.	98

Runs scored:

Mickey Mantle	N.Y.	119
Roger Maris	N.Y.	98
Minnie Minoso	Chi.	89
Jim Landis	Chi.	89
Roy Sievers	Chi.	87

Doubles:

Tito Francona	Cle.	36
Bill Skowron	N.Y.	34
Minnie Minoso	Chi.	32
Gene Freese	Chi.	32
	(3 tied with 31)	

Triples:

Nellie Fox	Chi.	10
Brooks Robinson	Balt.	9
	(5 tied with 7)	

Slugging Percentage:

Roger Maris	N.Y.	.581
Mickey Mantle	N.Y.	.558
Harmon Killebrew	Was.	.534
Roy Sievers	Chi.	.534
Bill Skowron	N.Y.	.528

On-Base Percentage:

Eddie Yost	Det.	.416
Gene Woodling	Balt.	.403
Pete Runnels	Bos.	.403
Mickey Mantle	N.Y.	.402
Roy Sievers	Chi.	.399

Bases on Balls:

Eddie Yost	Det.	125
Mickey Mantle	N.Y.	111
Bob Allison	Was.	92
Gene Woodling	Balt.	84
Jim Landis	Chi	80

Stolen Bases:

Luis Aparicio	Chi.	51
Jim Landis	Chi.	23
Lenny Green	Was.	21
Al Kaline	Det.	19
Jimmie Piersall	Cle.	18

Pitching

Wins:

Jim Perry	Cle.	18
Chuck Estrada	Balt.	18
Bud Daley	K.C.	16
	(3 tied with 15)	

Earned Run Average:

Frank Baumann	Chi.	2.68
Jim Bunning	Det.	2.79
Hal Brown	Balt.	3.06
Art Ditmar	N.Y.	3.06
Whitey Ford	N.Y.	3.08

Strikeouts:

Jim Bunning	Det.	201
Pedro Ramos	Was.	160
Early Wynn	Chi.	158
Frank Lary	Det.	149
Chuck Estrada	Balt.	144

Winning Percentage:

Jim Perry	Cle.	.643
Art Ditmar	N.Y.	.625
Chuck Estrada	Balt.	.621
Milt Pappas	Balt.	.577

Shutouts:

Early Wynn	Chi.	4
Jim Perry	Cle.	4
Whitey Ford	N.Y.	4
	(several tied with 3)	

Complete Games:

Frank Lary	Det.	15
Pedro Ramos	Was.	14
Ray Herbert	K.C.	14
Early Wynn	Chi.	13
Bud Daley	K.C.	13

Appearances:

Mike Fornieles	Bos.	70
Gerry Staley	Chi.	64
Tex Clevenger	Was.	53
Ray Moore	Chi., Was.	51
Marty Kutyna	K.C.	51

Innings Pitched:

Pedro Ramos	Was.	274
Frank Lary	Det.	274
Jim Perry	Cle.	261
Ray Herbert	K.C.	253
Jim Bunning	Det.	252

Appendix B

1960 Salaries of noteworthy major league players
(based on figures reported in various publications)

Ted Williams	$90,000
Willie Mays	$85,000
Stan Musial	$80,000
Warren Spahn	$72,500
Mickey Mantle	$66,000
Hank Aaron	$55,000
Yogi Berra	$50,000
Ernie Banks	$47,500
Minnie Minoso	$47,500
Eddie Mathews	$45,000
Harvey Kuenn	$44,500
Johnny Antonelli	$42,500
Al Kaline	$42,000
Frank Robinson	$40,000
Gil Hodges	$39,000
Duke Snider	$38,000
Luis Aparicio	$37,000
Ken Boyer	$35,000
Rocky Colavito	$35,000
Roy Face	$35,000
Whitey Ford	$35,000
Gene Woodling	$33,500
Gil McDougald	$33,000
Bob Friend	$32,500
Vern Law	$30,000
Don Hoak	$27,500

Orlando Cepeda	$27,000
Roberto Clemente	$22,500
Jim Bunning	$20,000
Harmon Killebrew	$20,000
Vada Pinson	$20,000
Hoyt Wilhelm	$19,500
Dick Groat	$18,000
Bill Mazeroski	$15,000

Appendix C

Complete Major League Rosters for 1960

National League

Chicago Cubs

Manager: Charlie Grimm (April–May)
Lou Boudreau (May–October)

George Altman	Jim Hegan
Bob Anderson	Al Heist
Richie Ashburn	Glen Hobbie
Earl Averill	Ben Johnson
Ernie Banks	Lou Johnson
Dick Bertell	Jerry Kindall
Ed Bouchee	Nelson Mathews
Jim Brewer	Jim McKnight
Dick Burwell	Seth Moreland
Don Cardwell	Walt Moryn
Art Ceccarelli	Danny Murphy
Moe Drabowsky	Cal Neeman
Dick Drott	Irv Noren
Dick Ellsworth	Del Rice
Don Elston	Ron Santo
Mark Freeman	John Schaffernorth
Dick Gernert	Al Schroll
John Goetz	Art Schult
Grady Hatton	El Tappe

Sammy Taylor
Tony Taylor
Moe Thacker
Frank Thomas

Bob Will
Billy Williams
Mel Wright
Don Zimmer

Cincinnati Reds

Manager: Fred Hutchinson
Rogelio Alvarez
Harry Anderson
Joe Azcue
Ed Bailey
Gus Bell
Marshall Bridges
Jim Brosnan
Leo Cardenas
Elio Chacon
Gordy Coleman
Cliff Cook
Dutch Dotterer
Joe Gaines
Tony Gonzalez
Bob Grim
Bill Henry
Jay Hook
Frank House
Willie Jones
Eddie Kasko

Brooks Lawrence
Whitey Lockman
Jerry Lynch
Jim Maloney
Billy Martin
Cal McLish
Roy McMillan
Don Newcombe
Joe Nuxhall
Jim O'Toole
Claude Osteen
Orlando Pena
Vada Pinson
Wally Post
Bob Purkey
Duane Richards
Frank Robinson
Raul Sanchez
Lee Walls
Ted Wieand
Pete Whisenant

Los Angeles Dodgers

Manager: Walt Alston
Sandy Amoros
Bob Aspromonte
Doug Camilli
Roger Craig
Tommy Davis
Willie Davis
Don Demeter
Don Drysdale
Chuck Essigian
Ron Fairly
Carl Furillo
Jim Gilliam
Jim Golden
Gil Hodges
Frank Howard
Sandy Koufax
Clem Labine
Norm Larker
Bob Lillis
Danny McDevitt
Wally Moon
Charlie Neal
Irv Noren
Phil Ortega
Ed Palmquist
Joe Pignatano
Johnny Podres
Ed Rakow
Rip Repulski
Ed Roebuck
John Roseboro
Larry Sherry
Norm Sherry
Charley Smith
Duke Snider
Stan Williams
Maury Wills

Milwaukee Braves

Manager: Chuck Dressen
Hank Aaron
Joe Adcock
Ray Boone
George Brunet
Bill Bruton
Bob Buhl
Lew Burdette
Chuck Cottier
Wes Covington
Del Crandall
Al Dark
Terry Fox
Len Gabrielson
Bob Giggie
Eddie Haas
Joey Jay
Mike Krsnich

Charlie Lau
Johnny Logan
Stan Lopata
Ken MacKenzie
Felix Mantilla
Eddie Mathews
Lee Maye
Don McMahon
Don Nottebart
Ron Piche

Juan Pizzaro
Mel Roach
Bob Rush
Red Schoendienst
Warren Spahn
Al Spangler
Frank Torre
Joe Torre
Carl Willey

Philadelphia Phillies

Manager: Eddie Sawyer
(April),
Andy Cohen (April),
Gene Mauch (April -
October)
Ruben Amaro
Harry Anderson
Ed Bouchee
John Buzhardt
Johhny Callison
Don Cardwell
Jimmie Coker
Gene Conley
Tony Curry
Clay Dalrymple
Al Dark
Boby Del Greco
Dick Farrell
Dallas Green
Ruben Gomez

Tony Gonzalez
Pancho Herrera
Joe Koppe
Ted Lepcio
Art Mahaffey
Bobby Malkmus
Hank Mason
Jack Meyer
Joe Morgan
Cal Neeman
Al Neiger
Jim Owens
Dave Phiiley
Taylor Phillips
Wally Post
Robin Roberts
Humberto Robinson
Chris Short
Curt Simmons
Bobby Gene Smith

Tony Taylor   Bobby Wine

Lee Walls   Jim Woods

Ken Walters

Pittsburgh Pirates

Manager: Danny Murtaugh	Don Hoak
Gene Baker	Danny Kravitz
Dick Barone	Clem Labine
Harry Bright	Vern Law
Smoky Burgess	Bill Mazeroski
Tom Cheney	Roman Mejias
Joe Christopher	Vinegar Bend Mizell
Gino Cimoli	Rocky Nelson
Robert Clemente	Bob Oldis
Bennie Daniels	Diomedes Olivo
Roy Face	Dick Schofield
Earl Francis	Bob Skinner
Bob Friend	Hal W. Smith
Joe Gibbon	R.C. Stevens
Paul Giel	Dick Stuart
Fred Green	Jim Umbricht
Dick Groat	Mickey Vernon
Don Gross	Bill Virdon
Harvey Haddix	George Witt

San Francisco Giants

Manager: Bill Rigney (April-June),	Dale Long
Tom Sheehan (June-October)	Georges Maranda
Felipe Alou	Juan Marichal
Matty Alou	Jim Marshall
Joey Amalfitano	Willie Mays
Johnny Antonelli	Mike McCormick
Don Blasingame	Willie McCovey
Ed Bressoud	Stu Miller
Bud Byerly	Ray Monzant
Orlando Cepeda	Billy O'Dell
Don Choate	Jose Pagan
Jim Davenport	Dave Philley
Eddie Fisher	Andre Rogers
Sam Jones	Jack Sanford
Sherman Jones	Bob Schmidt
Willie Kirkland	Joe Shipley
Hobie Landrith	Neil Wilson
Billy Loes	

St. Louis Cardinals

Manager: Solly Hemus	Doug Clemens
Frank Barnes	George Crowe
Ed Bauta	Joe Cunningham
Ken Boyer	Bob Duliba
Marshall Bridges	Curt Flood
Rocky Bridges	John Glenn
Ernie Broglio	Julio Gotay
Cal Browning	Alex Grammas
Ellis Burton	Dick Gray
Duke Carmel	Bob Grim
Chris Cannizaro	Larry Jackson

Charlie James
Julian Javier
Darrell Johnson
Ron Kline
Gary Kolb
Don Landrum
Tim McCarver
Lindy McDaniel
Bob Miller
Vinegar Bend Mizell
Walt Moryn
Stan Musial

Bob Nieman
Mel Nelson
Ed Olivares
Del Rice
Ray Sadecki
Bob Sadowski
Carl Sawatski
Wally Shannon
Curt Simmons
Hal R. Smith
Daryl Spencer
Leon Wagner
Bill White

American League

Baltimore Orioles

Manager: Paul Richards
Jerry Adair
John Anderson
Steve Barber
Ray Barker
Jackie Brandt
Marv Breeding
Bob Boyd
Hal Brown
Jim Busby
Rip Coleman
Clint Courtney
Walt Dropo
Chuck Estrada

Jack Fisher
Joe Ginsberg
Gene Green
Ron Hansen
Billy Hoeft
Gordon Jones
Billy Klaus
Bob Mabe
Dave Nicholson
Milt Pappas
Albie Pearson
Dave Philley
Al Pilarcik
Arnie Portocarrero

Johnny Powers
Del Rice
Brooks Robinson
Barry Shetrone
Gene Stephens
Wes Stock
Willie Tasby

Valmy Thomas
Bobby Thomson
Gus Triandos
Jerry Walker
Hoyt Wilhelm
Gene Woodling

Boston Red Sox

Manager: Billy Jurges
(April-June),
Del Baker (June),
Mike Higgins (June-
October)
Tom Borland
Ted Bowsfield
Tom Brewer
Don Buddin
Jim Busby
Jerry Casale
Nels Chittum
Lu Clinton
Marian Coughtry
Ike Delock
Arnold Early
Mike Fornieles
Gary Geiger
Don Gile
Pumpsie Green
Carroll Hardy
Dave Hillman
Ron Jackson

Marty Keough
Frank Malzone
Bill Monboquette
Billy Muffet
Chet Nichols
Russ Nixon
Jim Pagliaroni
Rip Repulski
Pete Runnels
Ed Sadowski
Tracy Stallard
Gene Stephens
Tom Sturdivant
Frank Sullivan
Haywood Sullivan
Willie Tasby
Bobby Thomson
Ray Webster
Vic Wertz
Ted Williams
Ted Wills
Earl Wilson
Al Worthington

Chicago White Sox

Manager: Al Lopez
Luis Aparicio
Earl Averill
Frank Baumann
Dick Brown
Cam Carreon
Dick Donovan
Sammy Esposito
Don Ferrarese
Nellie Fox
Gene Freese
Mike Garcia
Joe Ginsberg
Billy Goodman
Joe Hicks
Stan Johnson
Russ Kemmerer
Ted Kluszewski
Jim Landis
Sherm Lollar

Turk Lown
J.C. Martin
Ken McBride
Jim McAnany
Minnie Minoso
Ray Moore
Gary Peters
Billy Pierce
Jim Rivera
Floyd Robinson
Bob Rush
Herb Score
Bob Shaw
Roy Sievers
Al Smith
Gerry Staley
Jake Striker
Earl Torgeson
Al Worthington
Early Wynn

Cleveland Indians

Manager: Joe Gordon
(April-August),
Jo-Jo White (August),
Jimmie Dykes (August-
October)
Ken Aspromonte
Gary Bell
Walt Bond

Ted Bowsfield
Rocky Bridges
Johnny Briggs
Ty Cline
Mike de la Hoz
Steve Demeter
Don Dillard
Hank Foiles

Tito Francona
Frank Funk
Mudcat Grant
Bob Grim
Bob Hale
Carroll Hardy
Jack Harshman
Wynn Hawkins
Woody Held
Marty Keough
Johnny Klippstein
Harvey Kuenn
Barry Latman
Mike Lee
Bobby Locke
Carl Mathias
Joe Morgan

Don Newcombe
Russ Nixon
Jim Perry
Bubba Phillips
Jimmie Piersall
Vic Power
Johnny Powers
Johnny Romano
Dick Stigman
George Strickland
Chuck Tanner
Johnny Temple
Carl Thomas
Bobby Tiefenauer
Pete Whisenant
Red Wilson

Detroit Tigers

Manager: Jimmie Dykes
(April-August),
Billy Hitchcock (August)
Joe Gordon (August-
October)
Hank Aguirre
Sandy Amoros
Lou Berberet
Steve Bilko
Frank Bolling
Rocky Bridges
Bob Bruce
Jim Bunning

Pete Burnside
Norm Cash
Harry Chiti
Neil Chrisley
Rocky Colavito
Chico Fernandez
Bill Fischer
Hank Foiles
Paul Foytack
Dick Gernert
Johnny Groth
Gail Harris
Al Kaline

Clem Labine
Frank Lary
Em Limbeck
Charlie Maxwell
Dick McAuliffe
Tom Morgan
Don Mossi
Phil Regan

Ray Semproch
Dave Sisler
George Spencer
Coot Veal
Ozzie Virgil
Red Wilson
Eddie Yost

Kansas City Athletics

Manager: Bob Elliott
Hank Bauer
Ray Blemker
Chet Boak
Johnny Briggs
George Brunet
Andy Carey
Bob Cerv
Harry Chiti
Bud Daley
Pete Daley
Bob Davis
Jim Delsing
Hank Foiles
Ned Garver
Bob Giggie
Dick Hall
Ken Hamlin
Ray Herbert
Whitey Herzog
Ray Jablonski

Bob Johnson
Ken Johnson
Leo Kiely
Lou Klimchock
Danny Kravitz
Johnny Kucks
Marty Kutyna
Don Larsen
Jerry Lumpe
Jim McManus
Leo Posada
Howie Reed
Norm Siebern
Russ Snyder
Wayne Terwilliger
Marv Throneberry
Bob Trowbridge
John Tsitouris
Bill Tuttle
Dave Wickersham
Dick Williams

New York Yankees

Manager: Casey Stengel
Luis Arroyo
Yogi Berra
John Blanchard
Clete Boyer
Andy Carey
Bob Cerv
Jim Coates
Joe DeMaestri
Art Ditmar
Ryne Duren
Whitey Ford
John Gabler
Jesse Gonder
Eli Grba
Kent Hadley
Elston Howard
Ken Hunt
Johnny James

Deron Johnson
Fred Kipp
Tony Kubek
Dale Long
Hector Lopez
Duke Maas
Mickey Mantle
Roger Maris
Gil McDougald
Jim Pisoni
Bobby Richardson
Billy Shantz
Bobby Shantz
Bill Short
Bill Skowron
Bill Stafford
Hal Stowe
Ralph Terry
Bob Turley
Elmer Valo

Washington Senators

Manager: Cookie Lavagetto
Ted Abernathy
Bob Allison
Ken Aspromonte
Earl Battey
Julio Becquer
Reno Bertoia
Tex Clevenger
Billy Consolo

Dan Dobbek
Bill Fischer
Billy Gardner
Lenny Green
Rudy Hernandez
Dick Hyde
Lamar Jacobs
Jim Kaat
Russ Kemmerer

Harmon Killebrew

Jack Kralick

Don Lee

Jim Lemon

Hector Maestri

Don Mincher

Tom Morgan

Ray Moore

Hal Naragon

Camilo Pascual

Pedro Ramos

Ted Sadowski

John Schaive

Chuck Stobbs

Faye Throneberry

Elmer Valo

Jose Valdivielso

Zoilo Versalles

Pete Whisenant

Hal Woodeshick

Appendix D

Listing of 1960 Major League Umpires

National League

Al Barlick
Dusty Boggess
Ken Burkhart
Jocko Conlon
Hank Crawford
Frank Dascoli
Augie Donatelli
Tom Gorman
Bill Jackowski

Stan Landes
Chris Pelekoudas
Frank Secory
Vinnie Smith
Ed Sudol
Ed Vargo
Tony Venzon

American League

Charlie Berry
Nestor Chylak
Cal Drummond
John Flaherty
Jim Honochick
Ed Hurley
Bill Kinnamon
Bill McKinley
Larry Napp

Joe Papparella
John Rice
Ed Runge
Barry Schwarts
Al Smith
Hank Soar
John Stevens
Bob Stewart
Frank Umont

Appendix E

Chronological Listing of 1960 Major League Player Transactions

January 8   Cleveland traded Ray Webster to Boston for Leo Kiely.

January 9   Chicago signed free agent Chico Carrasquel.

January 11   Philadelphia traded Richie Ashburn to Chicago Cubs for Al Dark, Jim Woods, and John Buzhardt.

February 9   Braves signed free agent Stan Lopata.

March 29   Boston traded Jim Marshall to San Francisco for Al Worthington.

April 3   Baltimore traded Billy Gardner to Washington for Clint Courtney and Ron Samford.

April 4   Chicago White Sox traded Earl Battey and Don Mincher plus cash to Washington for Roy Sievers.

April 5   San Francisco purchased Dale Long from Chicago Cubs.

April 5   Kansas City traded Bob Grim to Cleveland for Leo Kiely.

April 5   New York traded two minor leaguers to Los Angeles for Fred Kipp.

April 8   Los Angeles traded Don Zimmer to Chicago Cubs for three minor leaguers and cash.

April 11   Cleveland purchased Johnny Klippstein from Dodgers.

April 12   Detroit traded Steve Demeter to Cleveland for Norm Cash.

April 17   Detroit traded Harvey Kuenn to Cleveland for Rocky Colavito.

April 18   Cleveland traded Herb Score to Chicago White Sox for Barry Latman.

April 29	Cleveland purchased Pete Whisenant from Cincinnati.
May 6	Los Angeles traded Rip Repulski to Boston for Nelson Chittum.
May 6	Los Angeles traded Sandy Amoros to Detroit for Gail Harris.
May 11	Milwaukee traded Bob Giggie to Kansas City for George Brunet.
May 12	San Francisco purchased Dave Philley from Philadelphia.
May 12	Cleveland purchase John Powers from Baltimore.
May 13	Philadelphia traded Ed Bouchee and Don Cardwell to Chicago Cubs for Tony Taylor and Cal Neeman.
May 15	Washington traded Ken Aspromonte to Cleveland for Pete Whisenant.
May 17	Milwaukee traded Ray Boone to Boston for Ron Jackson.
May 17	Chicago White Sox purchased Russ Kemmerer from Washington.
May 18	Cincinnati purchased Bob Grim from Cleveland.
May 19	New York traded Andy Carey to Kansas City for Bob Cerv.
May 20	St. Louis signed free agent Curt Simmons.
May 24	Washington signed free agent Elmer Valo.
May 27	St. Louis traded Vinegar Bend Mizell and Dick Gray to Pittsburgh for Julian Javier and Ed Bauta.
May 31	Pittsburgh traded Danny Kravitz to Kansas City Hank Foiles. Foiles was then traded to Cleveland for John Powers.
June 7	Los Angeles signed free agent Irv Noren.
June 9	Baltimore traded Willie Tasby to Boston for Gene Stephens.
June 11	Chicago White Sox purchased Bob Rush from Milwaukee.

June 13	Cleveland traded Russ Nixon and Carroll Hardy to Boston for Marty Keough and Ted Bowsfield.
June 13	Washington purchased Ray Moore from White Sox.
June 15	Chicago Cubs traded Walt Moryn to St. Louis for Jim McKnight and cash.
June 15	Los Angeles traded Clem Labine to Detroit for Ray Semproch and cash.
June 15	Cincinnati traded Tony Gonzalez and Lee Walls to Philadelphia for Wally Post, Harry Anderson, and Fred Hopke.
June 15	St. Louis traded Jim Donohue to Los Angeles for John Glenn.
June 18	Chicago signed free agent Joe Ginsberg.
June 23	Philadelphia traded Al Dark to Milwaukee for Joe Morgan.
July 4	Baltimore signed free agent Bobby Thomson.
July 22	Detroit traded Tom Morgan to Washington for Bill Fischer.
July 25	Cleveland traded Hank Foiles to Detroit for Bob Wilson and Rocky Bridges.
July 26	Detroit purchased Harry Chiti from Kansas City.
July 29	St. Louis purchased Bob Grim from Cincinnati.
July 29	Cleveland purchased Don Newcombe from Cincinnati.
July 30	Kansas City purchased Johnny Briggs from Cleveland.
August 2	Cincinnati purchased Marshall Bridges from St. Louis.
August 9	Cleveland purchased Joe Morgan from Philadelphia.
August 16	Pittsburgh signed free agent Clem Labine.
August 22	New York purchased Dale Long from San Francisco.
August 31	Detroit purchased Dick Gernert from Chicago Cubs.
September 1	Baltimore purchased Dave Philley from San Francisco.

September 2 St. Louis purchased Rocky Bridges from Cleveland.

October 31 San Francisco traded Andre Rodgers to Milwaukee for Al Dark, who was immediately named as Giants manager.

November 28 Milwaukee purchased Dick Brown from Chicago White Sox.

December 3 Cleveland traded Harvey Kuenn to San Francisco for Johnny Antonelli and Willie Kirkland.

December 3 Milwaukee purchased Billy Martin from Cincinnati.

December 7 Detroit traded Frank Bolling and a player to be named later to Milwaukee for Bill Bruton, Chuck Cottier, Dick Brown, and Terry Fox.

December 15 Milwaukee traded Joey Jay and Juan Pizarro to Cincinnati for Roy McMillan and a player to be named later.

December 15 Cincinnati traded Cal McLish and Juan Pizarro to Chicago White Sox for Gene Freese.

December 15 Baltimore purchased Earl Robinson from Los Angeles Dodgers.

December 15 Philadelphia traded Gene Conley to Boston for Frank Sullivan.

December 16 Washington traded Bobby Shantz to Pittsburgh for Bennie Daniels, R. C. Stevens, and Harry Bright.

December 16 Los Angeles Dodgers traded Danny McDevitt to New York for cash and a player to be named later.

December 29 Kansas City traded Marty Kutyna and cash to Washington for Haywood Sullivan.

Bibliography

Books

Brosnan, Jim. (1960). *The Long Season.* Harper and Row.

Honig, Donald. (1987). *The All-Star Game.* The Sporting News.

Honig, Donald. (1990). *The Boston Red Sox.* Prentice Hall Press.

Lowry, Philip. (1992). *Green Cathedrals.* Addison Wesley.

Fiorito, Len, and Marazzi, Rich. (1982). *Aaron to Zuverink.* Avon.

Cohen, Richard, and Neft, David. (1985). *The Sports Encyclopedia 6th edition.* St. Martin's.

Cohen, Richard, and Neft, David. (1990). *The World Series.* St. Martin's.

Redmount, Robert. (1998). *The Red Sox Encyclopedia.* Sports Publishing.

Reichler, Joseph.(1986). *Baseball's Greatest Moments.* Bonanza Books.

Palmer, Pete with Reuther, David, and Thorn, John. (1989). *Total Baseball.* Warner Books.

(1996). *The Baseball Encyclopedia.* Macmillan tenth edition.

(1986). *Cooperstown—Where the Legends Live Forever.* Arlington House.

(1989). *The Official NBA Basketball Encyclopedia.* Villard.

(1992). *20th Century Baseball Chronicle.* Publications International Ltd.

(1985). *Topps Baseball Cards.* Warner Books.

(1960). *Baseball Official Guide.* The Sporting News.

(1961). *Baseball Official Guide.* The Sporting News.

(1997). *The National Pastime.* S.A.B.R..

Magazines

The Sporting News
Sports Illustrated
Sport
Saturday Evening Post

Newspapers

New York Times
Boston Globe
Boston Herald

Index

VISIT OUR WEBSITE

www.

At

www.sportspublishinginc.com

.com

ADDITIONAL TITLES FROM SPORTS PUBLISHING INC.

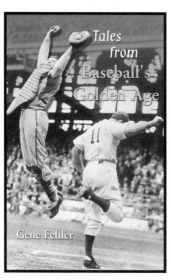

Tales from Baseball's Golden Age
By Gene Fehler

Tales from Baseball's Golden Age takes a trip down memory lane by relaying anecdotes from players of the 1940s and '50s. With Tim McCarver, Ralph Kiner, Bobby Thomson, and many other legends interviewed for the collection, it promises to be a book that can't be put down.

5 1/2 X 8 1/4 hardcover • 200 pages $19.95

Crack of the Bat
The Louisville Slugger Story
By Bob Hill

Crack of the Bat: The Louisville Slugger Story is a comprehensive and entertaining look at a baseball icon, the Louisville Slugger bat. With full-color photos of baseball legends, icons, and decals, *Crack of the Bat* is a keepsake that will be cherished as much as some of the bats it describes.

9 X 12 hardcover • 160 pages • $29.95

To Order: Call 1-877-424-BOOK (2665) or
For Savings, Service, and Speedy Delivery, Order On-Line At:
www.sportspublishinginc.com